Sojourn with Heidi

Heidi Fearon - 18 months old, 1941

HEIDI LEITNER FEARON

authorHOUSE

AuthorHouse™
1663 Liberty Drive
Bloomington, IN 47403
www.authorhouse.com
Phone: 1 (800) 839-8640

© 2020 Heidi Leitner Fearon. All rights reserved.

No part of this book may be reproduced, stored in a retrieval system, or transmitted by any means without the written permission of the author.

Published by AuthorHouse 02/17/2020

ISBN: 978-1-7283-4638-0 (sc)
ISBN: 978-1-7283-4639-7 (hc)
ISBN: 978-1-7283-4637-3 (e)

Print information available on the last page.

Any people depicted in stock imagery provided by Getty Images are models, and such images are being used for illustrative purposes only.
Certain stock imagery © Getty Images.

This book is printed on acid-free paper.

Because of the dynamic nature of the Internet, any web addresses or links contained in this book may have changed since publication and may no longer be valid. The views expressed in this work are solely those of the author and do not necessarily reflect the views of the publisher, and the publisher hereby disclaims any responsibility for them.

Contents

Dedication to my Parents vii
Preface: My Story ix

Chapter 1   Getting to Know My Family 1
Chapter 2   The Things I Remember about the War 4
Chapter 3   After the War—A New Beginning 7
Chapter 4   Now I Go to Paris... 15
Chapter 5   A New Adventure in Cambridge, England................... 27
Chapter 6   Back to Salzburg but for How Long? 33
Chapter 7   America, Here I Come.. 36
Chapter 8   Road Trip to Montreal.. 43
Chapter 9   Now Back to the Real World 53
Chapter 10   Fred Leaving Time Magazine to Start CHIMO
             Magazine 58
Chapter 11   An Old Friendship Evolves—Cal................................. 64
Chapter 12   A New Start.. 68
Chapter 13   Now the Big Boat 72
Chapter 14   Selling the Suburban Gas Company 77
Chapter 15   The Caribbean 1500 82
Chapter 16   We Are Off Again... 88
Chapter 17   Sailing the Caribbean Islands 92
Chapter 18   Sailing the Leeward Islands—Anguilla to Dominica....... 96
Chapter 19   A Season in Grenada...103
Chapter 20   Bermuda, Here We Come... 106
Chapter 21   Testing Our Survival Skills.. 108
Chapter 22   Back to Syracuse, 1994 113
Chapter 23   Following the Wind..119

Chapter 24	The Passing of My Mom	121
Chapter 25	Return to Cal and the Good Life	122
Chapter 26	The US Virgins (Islands!)	126
Chapter 27	Concerns regarding Cal's Health	130
Chapter 28	Cal's Diagnosis Is Confirmed—Finding a Home on Hilton Head	132
Chapter 29	Cal's Passing—September 24, 1998	135
Chapter 30	Getting the Boat Ready for Sale	139
Chapter 31	A Very Special Day—A Buyer for the Boat	141
Chapter 32	My New Life on Hilton Head as a Bachelorette	144
Chapter 33	The Hilton Head Island Experience	145
Chapter 34	Life Goes On	149
Chapter 35	My Love for Hilton Head Island	152

About the Author 157

Dedication to my Parents

The name on my birth certificate is Heidegunde (now Heidi) Alrune Hildegard Leitner. I was born three weeks early, small but healthy. I was born a very lucky girl.

I had the most loving parents anybody could ever imagine. Because of their love, encouragement, and patience, I grew more and more confident at each stage of my life. Because of them, I believed I could do anything. I still feel the same way today.

I learned very early in life to love and respect others, particularly my parents. They were strict but always loving. I did my chores without complaint. I never talked back to my parents. The chores assigned to me when I was a child, like weeding the vegetable garden, making my bed, cleaning my room, washing dishes, cleaning my shoes, and doing homework, taught me self-discipline and how to eventually become an independent woman.

Expressing thanks and showing my appreciation to family and friends involved sending thank-you notes. I was around six years old when I learned to write thank-you notes. This was all about teaching respect and good manners. We made our own cards, and of course, Mom helped me with everything. She and I would walk together to the mailbox and deposit the envelope in the mail. My reward for my effort was a big hug from Mom. Today I still write thank-you notes.

Times may have been hard after the war, but I don't remember life that way. My mother always found a way to provide for us and made it fun. She made us understand that there are things that we all want, but what's most important in life is the love we share and what is in our hearts. She also said that whatever you give will come back to you. And it did!

Mom was a stay-at-home mom, but she was well known for the books and poetry that she wrote. To this day, I receive an income from her books and poetry.

I was always encouraged to keep a diary, to write things down, to record my impressions and memories. My mom kept all my diaries. Mom was thirty years a widow. She started traveling and continued her love and passion for writing. Writing your thoughts down does do wonders with regard to reflecting on your life. Like my mother, I kept meticulous records of the significant events in my life. The diaries that my mother kept as well as my diaries, photos, paintings, news articles, and historic memorabilia helped me immensely in writing my memoirs.

Also, thank you to my dad for giving me the coin I mention in my story. I have since learned that the coin is very valuable, and I am wearing it right now.

So Mom and Dad, thank you again for the great job you did in giving me confidence and courage and enabling me to be the master of my own life.

Have respect for the life that has been given to you, and guide it with your heart.

Preface: My Story

My name is Heidi Leitner Fearon. I was born in Salzburg, Austria, in 1940. My parents were educated and always encouraged my brother and me to live our lives to the fullest. Life has offered me so many opportunities, and in most cases, I have chosen the path less traveled. And so there have been many adventures. I have decided to chronicle many of the events in my life, the happy and the sad, and share them with you. The experiences I've had and the lessons I've learned will be familiar. But it's how you apply these lessons that will bring great joy to your life. I am now living in Hilton Head Island, South Carolina, which I call paradise. It has been my home for the past twenty-one years. I am so thankful that I am able to enjoy every day of my life on this island. I hope you find my stories entertaining, thought-provoking, and full of good humor.

This book was written for my son, Scott, whom I treasure. He is now the proud father of my grandson, Victor. I'd also like to share my experiences with all the young people who would like to travel throughout the world but can't imagine affording to live such a dream. I would like to tell you my story and how I got here. But first let me tell you about my first family—young Heidi, my mom, and my dad.

1

Getting to Know My Family

My father was born in Austria in 1899. My mother was born near Berlin, Germany, in 1903. My father was one of eight brothers, six of whom lost their lives in World War II. My father and my uncle Julius were the only two surviving siblings. Losing six sons had a devastating effect on my grandfather. As a result of these losses, my grandfather committed suicide. This all happened before I was born.

I have no memories of my grandparents except for a picture of my father's mother holding me when I was four months old. She passed away shortly after the picture was taken.

My parents met in 1932 on the lake Chiemsee in Germany. My mother was attending sailing school. All the girls had passed their sailing test, and Adolf Hitler invited all of the girls to visit him in his house in Berchtesgaden. The girls were all lined up, dressed in their white sailing uniforms. Hitler congratulated every one of them and shook their hands. My mother wrote an article in the local newspaper about this event. I have photographs of this grandiose affair.

Well, as you can guess, my mother and father fell very much in love after their first meeting at the lake. After corresponding for two years, they decided to get married!

Before my mother met my father, she worked at a children's home as a child psychologist. She loved her job and also enjoyed taking dance lessons after work. She was earning a good salary. In fact, she had a very lovely life. But she decided to give it all up to marry my father.

My father's life before he married was also very interesting. He was an architect. He went to Rio de Janeiro in 1926 to work on a very large project, the construction of the Copacabana Plaza.

My parents were married in 1934. It was a very big day! Because of the political situation in Germany, it was difficult for a German to marry an Austrian. My parents had to marry at the Austrian–German border. My grandfather and my mother's brothers and sisters all came to the border to say goodbye. Once she left Germany, my mother would not be allowed to return. She had to give up her German passport.

After the war, my father continued to work as an architect and builder. His brother Julius was a medical doctor and my very favorite uncle.

I was born in 1940, during the war years. I had a brother who was two years older than me. My mother was a writer and published her first book the year my brother was born. The birth of a healthy baby boy was a major event, noteworthy to Adolf Hitler. Because I was a girl, my birth was less dramatic. I just quietly came along. However, my mom told me I was a great joy to her. She told me she had a very easy pregnancy with me, in contrast to her pregnancy with my brother, Manfred.

Sojourn with Heidi

My father in Rio de Janeiro, Copa Cabana Beach, 1926.

The Sailing School in Chiemsee was invited to have pastry and coffee with Adolf Hilter in Berschtesgaden, 1933.

2

The Things I Remember about the War

I was only three or four, but I still remember the sound of the sirens. Whenever we heard the sirens, we all had to pack up our things and go into the mountain. The mountain was called Mönchsberg. So many times, daytime and nighttime, we had to go to the shelter.

During this time, my mom made me a little doll. The eyes were two little buttons, the hair was made of pieces of wool, and my mother embroidered lips onto the face. Actually, she was not that pretty, but she was the only doll I had! One night we were running to the mountain. There were so many people running down the street. Some had little packages they were holding tight, and I had my doll. With all the rushing and confusion, I somehow lost my doll. I was crying uncontrollably. At first my mother thought I was crying because Dad was at war or because I had hurt myself. But through my tears she heard me saying, "No, no, no, it's my doll. I lost my doll!"

We never found the doll. After seeing me so sad, my mom managed to make me a new doll. Now when the sirens would ring and we had to go to the mountains, the doll stayed at home.

I also remember the water reservoir in our town. It was bombed, so there was no water coming directly to the houses. The town had a common well at the bottom of the street. Everybody went there to get drinking water. I was so small that I couldn't carry much. My mom would say, "The more water you bring home, the more hugs I'll give you." I remember taking many trips to that well.

My father came home on leave one night when the sirens were ringing.

Sojourn with Heidi

He decided we'd go into the cellar and wait for the bombing to stop. A bomb hit the small mountain next to our house. I will never forget the air pressure from the explosion. It caused most of the windows in the house to break. The sound of breaking glass was unbelievable. I will never forget that sound. There were many deaths from that event, and we were lucky to have survived.

Growing up in Austria during the war was not easy for many people. The men were at war, and the women were raising the children and caring for their homes. I saw my father for the first time when I was about three years old. He was always smiling. He made lots of toys for us out of cigar boxes or thread spools or whatever he could find. He also loved to sing. He got up very early every day and began singing right away. I hated it, but nevertheless, he made everybody smile. And then he was gone again.

During his administration, Hitler did one good thing for women. Every school-age young lady had to spend one year in a household with children (the young women were called *Pflichtjahrmädchen*) to help learn how to care for a house and help raise the children. This was a great help to moms. My mother was an author and appreciated the girls' help. It gave her more time to write her stories on her typewriter. Even when I had my nap in the afternoon, I could hear my mom on the typewriter. I will never forget her very black, very big, very ugly typewriter and the sounds that it made.

Do I remember hard times? Maybe there were some. But I never remember being hungry or cold. There were always things we wanted, things we had difficulty getting, but somehow they'd finally arrive, and everyone would be so happy and appreciative that we would forget about the long wait.

My mother had no problem providing me with shoes—my brother's shoes were always passed on to me! I remember wanting a pair of shoes of my own only one time. I saw a pair of felt boots in a neighbor's window next to a sign saying they were for sale. I wanted them so badly that I dreamed about them.

It was springtime, really too late in the season to buy boots. My mother tried so hard to talk me out of buying them. But I persisted, and my mother finally agreed. We went to see the nice lady down the street, and I was allowed to try on the boots. The lady asked me if there was room for growth. I said they felt sooo big! All was going well until we started to discuss the price. This nice lady wanted three dozen eggs for the boots!

We had chickens in our garden that we used for food and to trade. An egg was a very precious thing. We traded eggs for my brother's piano lessons, and God knows what else was on the list. My mother tried reasoning with me: "These are white boots—who is going to keep them clean? And we have so little soap for our clothing, and now we'll be using precious soap to clean a pair of white felt boots?"

I jumped onto my mother's lap and gave her the biggest hug and kiss. I said, "Mom, I will clean them myself." I told her that every day I'd bring the nice lady my egg. I would not eat my share of eggs until it was time to take the boots home.

My mom's heart softened, and she said, "Okay, Heidi, but are you sure they will fit you by next winter?"

"I am sure, Mutti. They are so big!"

The kind lady selling the boots had a tear rolling down her cheek. She told me that she would only charge me two and a half dozen eggs; that would be fine. I had to ask the lady one more thing—to please keep the boots in the window so I could look at them each day until I took them home. She was smiling when we left.

One of my greatest memories is bringing the lady the last egg and bringing home my new boots, though they were actually not new at all—they were her daughter's.

It was September, my birthday, and I felt like I was in heaven when I got the boots. Nobody could have been happier than I was! However, Mom had been right: the boots were tight, too tight, so I wore them with the skinniest socks. Even so, they did hurt my feet. When I had my Saturday bath, Mom noticed the blisters on my feet. I had to admit to her that the boots were too small. Still, I cleaned them every day, knowing they'd soon be traded for something else. I sure did a great selling job. Everybody wanted the white boots after I was through cleaning them!

3

After the War—A New Beginning

My dad came home in September 1945. The war in Europe ended on September 2. The official date for the USA was May 8, 1945.

I was five years old when my father returned home from the war and life started to return to normal. We resumed all of our family activities and enjoyed all of our friends in the neighborhood. We had a sled and enjoyed tobogganing. We went skiing (which is still one of my favorite sports). As some might remember, we had ice skates that screwed onto our winter boots. We had only one pair of boots, which we wore to school as well as for skating and skiing. We had the best time growing up.

In winter our clothes were always soaking wet, and Mom was always knitting to keep up with our need for gloves, hats, scarves, leggings, and sweaters! My mother saved old knitted items so that she could resize and recreate clothing. Christmas was always a surprise. We received a new sweater every year. She'd refit an old sweater and make it larger by adding a new color and changing the design. She once made me a new winter coat from an old army blanket. It was great, and life was wonderful! We grew up with all the love and happiness imaginable.

My mother had a big Singer sewing machine and made all our clothes. I was fascinated by the machine but was too young to use it. I had to wait for my legs to grow longer so my feet could reach the pedal. Once that happened, she would teach me how to sew. Because of Mom's skills, I always had something new to wear.

One day we received a big parcel sent from California. It was from my mother's oldest sister, Grete. She had married before the war and moved to California. I was so excited that I wanted to open it right away! But no, my father had us wait until we had finished eating dinner, then finished washing the dishes and finally putting the dishes away. Only now would we sit around the box with great anticipation.

This was a great moment for all of us—a package from America! My father carefully opened the box. The first thing I noticed was some pretty paper with a letter on top. Of course, the letter had to be read first. My mother read the letter and started to cry. I asked why she was crying, and she said, "I am just so happy."

As Dad removed the paper and carefully folded it, we could see a jar. It was peanut butter! I had never seen anything like this before. There was also a package of flour, another of sugar, and a container of Crisco. In a little paper bag, there were four chocolate bars. The wrappers said "Butterfinger." There was one more present for my mother, a pair of nylon stockings. We all gave each other a big hug and danced around the room. This was better than any Christmas! I wanted to know, what is Butterfinger? Well, when I had a tiny piece of Butterfinger, I thought I had died and gone to heaven. It was rationed out for a long time. But my wish was one day to visit the Butterfinger country. I was only six years old, but that was my future plan! My aunt and uncle sent us many more parcels, and every time it was like Christmas.

When my brother was six years old, my father managed to find a child's violin for him. He kept it a secret until my brother's birthday. It was in a black case and was tied with a blue ribbon. When my brother opened the case, he asked, "What do I do with it?"

"Well, Manfred," my father said, "you are now six years old, and we would like you to learn to play the violin."

My mother was sitting with her hands folded, thinking, *Maybe he will be another Mozart.* She didn't notice the big tear rolling down his cheek. He jumped into my mother's lap and cried (which he did often).

My mother asked, "What is the matter?"

Manfred answered, "I don't like it!" My mother played the piano, and that was the instrument he wanted to play.

As usual, he got his way! I still have to laugh about the whole situation. However, this was not the end of the violin story. Two years later, I turned six years old, and now it was my turn. To soften the blow, my mother gave me a doll. She also made a pretty dress for the doll, from the fabric used for my crib skirt when I was a baby. Believe me, nothing was ever wasted. Now I was faced with the violin predicament. No, I did not cry. I said I would give it a try. A Mozart was now out of the question, but maybe I could be a future Nannerl, the sister of Mozart!

Times were still hard, but with some sacrifices, I was enrolled in the Salzburg Mozarteum. I had to practice my violin one hour every day. As I got older, my father found an adult violin for me to play. After homework and now the violin, there was not much time left to just play! I am sure when I had to practice my violin, there was no mouse in the house. Even the neighbors' dog started howling like a hyena when I attacked my instrument. But I did get better and started to enjoy playing. On Christmas and other holidays, my brother played the piano with my mom, I played the violin, and my father sang at the top of his voice. We had a great time, a little like the Von Trapp family!

I liked to improvise when playing the violin, but my teacher said that was a no-no. I was told to follow the music exactly as it was written. There were times when I wondered, *Will I ever be free from this violin?* After years of practice, I actually got quite good, but it was not for me. When I went off to live in Paris, I did not take my violin. Sometimes I think I went to Paris just to get rid of playing the violin!

I was six years old when I started the first grade. Although there never seemed to be enough money for everything, my mother found a way to send me to ballet school, and I loved every minute of it. The class was taught in the local theater, and my teacher was Frau Kammer. She was an older lady, herself a ballerina, and was still a very good dancer. The discipline was what I liked most about dancing. Every movement had to be just right. Sometimes after practice I'd be so sore, but I had to endure it. My love of dancing inspired me, and I trained hard for fifteen years. Finally, everything seemed to come together. I even walked like a dancer. My toes would point to the outside, and my arms gracefully glided beside my body. I remember jumping and dancing home after my lessons. Of course, there was no car waiting for me. Walking was my primary means of transportation!

I was seven when I first started to sketch and create ideas for clothes. I was very young but very creative. So many of my designs were of dresses that I wanted for myself. Mom laughed at me because some of these drawings were impossible for us to make or not suitable for me to wear.

Drawing clothes and my love for fabric eventually led me to the design school in Salzburg. I entered the school when I was fourteen and completed the program at age eighteen. I loved working with fabric. School was my opportunity to learn how to design a dress the right way. I would soon have a practical profession.

My brother attended the university in Graz, Austria. This was a great expense for my father. My education in design was the right choice for me, and I happened to love it.

I was eight years old when an American family came to live with us. After the war, the American military arranged for American families to live with Austrian families. The couple lived upstairs in our big house with their little girl, Theresa. One day the American family smuggled me into the American military campus. It was called Camp Schröder, and you could enter only if you were American military. The family had a big car and told me to hide on the floor under a blanket.

When I was told to get up, I could not believe where I was! It was like another world! The family introduced me to football, held at the base, and this was where I had my first taste of popcorn and, later, my first ice cream ever! Hearing English spoken by everyone was a new experience for me. I told my parents about all of this, and they couldn't believe it either.

Gradually, I learned more English words, and Theresa learned more German words, so communication was never a problem for us. I think the American family stayed with us for three years. It was great! My father liked the American father. They managed to find a way to communicate, often aided by some Austrian schnapps. With school, my American friends, dancing, and playing the violin, I was very busy. The years just flew by!

The American family introduced me to a Sears catalog. I was in awe of all the beautiful dresses. It was hard for me to believe that you could actually order these dresses, and they would then be shipped to you. I was allowed to cut out one page. I thought the dress on this page was the most beautiful of them all, blue with lace around the neck. I wrapped this page as a Christmas present and gave it to my mom. I think I knew I would one day design a dress for her.

The Sears catalog was a wonderful experience. I remember being

Sojourn with Heidi

allowed to choose one item from the catalog. I chose a small blow-up pool for the garden, and all my friends came to my house to see and use it. I have a picture of Theresa and my neighbors in that little pool.

I was about nine years old when my father wanted me to take riding lessons from his friend in the military. The major was a superb teacher. You should know that my father was not at all in favor of my dancing, but he wanted me to have riding instructions. However, in return for the lessons, I had to help groom the horses. My first lesson took place without a saddle. Because of my ballet training, my legs were very strong. But without a saddle, the inside of my thighs was very sore after riding. But I got better and better. I loved riding!

Being around horses so much created a problem. I could not tell Frau Kammer that I was riding horses. I was a dancer! Sometimes it was hard to get rid of the horse smell. Some days, she'd say, "Heidi, you smell like a horse!" I had to be very careful and find a way to get rid of the horse smell.

In addition to school, my American friends, ballet, and violin, I now had riding lessons! I should mention that my father was a very good skier and also was teaching me to ski—as if there wasn't enough for me to do! At age fourteen, I passed the test to become a ski instructor. I taught children how to ski and loved doing it.

When I was growing up, my mother and dad were acutely aware of my talents and interests and offered me every opportunity to pursue them. I wanted to learn everything—how to design clothes, how to dance, how to ride and ski. My enthusiasm for life was endless.

My mother danced when she was young. It was a type of modern dance, a kind of free body expression. Her back was very flexible, in a way mine was not. I think deep down inside, my mother really wanted to be a dancer. I loved the exercise and discipline associated with dancing, but I had no desire to become a professional dancer.

When I was in my mid-teens, ballet classes provided many opportunities for me. The theater offered ballet students walk-on parts in various plays and operas. I acted in two movies. My father did not like the idea of my having any kind of acting job. I was offered a small part in a movie titled *Liebe Sommer und Musik*, directed by Otto Preminger. As part of the movie, my character was to kiss a boy as he walked out of a tent. Mr. Preminger gave the direction for me to kiss the boy, but I just said no. Well, that was the end of my film career. All the other girls raised their hands and said, "I will do it, I will do it!" My only thought was that if my father saw me kissing a boy in a movie, he would not like it.

I had no real interest in being an actress, but it was a good way to earn money. I had a different plan. Once I finished design school, I wanted to go to Paris! My mother was my best friend and confidant, and the dream of going to Paris was a mother-daughter secret. I saved all the money I made for my trip to Paris.

At this time in her life, my mother's career was taking off. She had published her first book, *In Tanzt*, in 1938 in Salzburg, Austria. This was a great year for her, given that it also was the year my brother was born.

In 1956, my mother wrote a book titled *Im Zeichen des Feuers*. The story was originally titled "Schinderbarbele" and published as a series in a local newspaper. It was also performed as a stage play. She did the research for the book over a ten-year period. It was a true story about a redheaded woman, Barbara Koller, who could heal people with herbs and roots. The healings occurred only during full moons. In the end she was burned to death because she was thought to be a witch. I had a small part in the play, playing the witch's daughter. Of course, the money I made was stashed away for my Paris trip. The later book version titled *Im Zeichen des Feuers* was her masterpiece. The book is still popular and selling.

Of course, there are always some exceptions to one's savings plans. I really needed to buy a bicycle, my first! I had to make payments for the bike over a six-month period. When all the payments were made, I had a new means of transportation. I was so happy to ride my bike home from the shop. It was blue and had three gears and a lock. I never asked my parents for help. They were so proud of me when I came home with my new bike.

In the midst of my teen years, we bought a German shepherd named Telly, and he soon became a very special member of the family. One of his ears stood tall while the other just dropped down. We all loved that dog.

During this same time, we reconsidered the need for our chicken coop. We didn't have chickens anymore, so why not make the chicken coop my dollhouse? It was a long time before we were rid of the chicken smell, but it was my dollhouse, and that was all that mattered!

When I was fourteen and my brother was sixteen, my father built a restaurant just down the street from where we lived. The restaurant also had a disco bar in the basement. Of course, my brother, being two years older than me, was allowed to go to the restaurant, but I was not. My brother told me about the jukebox playing music and everybody dancing to rock and roll. I asked him if he would take me, and we made a plan! My brother would put a ladder against the wall of the house, and I would climb out my window. We had to wait until my father was asleep, which meant listening for the sound of his snoring. My brother tied a fishing line to my toe and stretched it to his bedroom so we could make contact. When he heard my father snoring, my brother pulled on the line to alert me to get ready. I then locked my bedroom door from the inside while my brother steadied the ladder for me to climb down.

I will never forget that disco night. All our friends went to a dance school to learn to waltz, but dancing to rock and roll music was different. We all had such a good time together, and my father never found out!

My brother Manfred and me, 1947.

Heidi Leitner Fearon

My doll, 1942.

Theresa in my first catalog pool and friends, 1950.

4

Now I Go to Paris

It was just a usual day. The family had a nice lunch. My father enjoyed a beer and, like every day, an afternoon siesta. As he was awaking, I jumped onto the sofa, saying, "I have something to tell you!"

"Okay, Heidi, what is it?"

I didn't want him to be angry. I just wanted him to know that I was going to Paris.

He said, "You are doing what?"

I said, "You heard me all right. I found an au pair job with a very nice family. I will be going to school every day and will have the opportunity to learn to speak French! I'll see lots of beautiful clothes, and I'll learn so much more about fashion!" I told him I had a return train ticket, and I'd be able to come back anytime I wanted.

He said, "I'm not angry, Rube," using his nickname for me, meaning "Carrot." "I just can't believe that you are growing up. Please promise to be good and nice to everyone. I know you'll be back very soon. I give you my blessing."

"Thank you, thank you, Daddy! I promised to be good and to never disappoint you!"

I went to see my mom in the garden. "Well, Heidi, how did it go?" she asked.

At first I didn't say a word. Then I started to cry. My mother gave me a hug. She said, "This is not the end of the world. One day Dad will understand."

Heidi Leitner Fearon

Now I had to tell my father, 1957.

"But Mom, he said yes!" I was so elated that I had tears running down my cheeks.

"Oh, Heidi," she said, "I am so happy for you." She had tears in her eyes as well.

I hadn't had time to tell him I was leaving in two weeks. Now I was really going to have to pack that monster suitcase! At that time, we didn't have wheels on our luggage. I had to decide what to take and how to pack, and I had to be able to carry everything with me! I made a list of everything I wanted to take. I packed and unpacked so many times, but there was still so much I wanted to take with me.

The two weeks went by very fast. Soon it was New Year's Eve, and we had a wonderful evening! We all went to see the fireworks. All my friends were there, hugging one another as we said our goodbyes.

The date of my departure was January 2, 1959. Mom and Dad stood on the platform as I boarded the overnight train to Paris. I was both sad and happy when we said our goodbyes. When my father carried that

Sojourn with Heidi

monster bag to my compartment and put it on an overhead shelf, he asked me, "Heidi, are you sure you packed enough?"

I said, "I'm not sure, but I think I packed all the essentials." I had what I thought I needed.

The train whistled, and all the doors were shut. I opened the window to wave goodbye. As the train slowly started to move, I could no longer see anybody. I shut the window and sat down in my assigned seat. I had no idea what was ahead of me, but it was all very exciting! I was surprised to discover that there were five other people in the compartment with me. I folded my hands and shut my eyes. A new chapter of my life was about to begin!

My mother had packed me a sandwich for lunch as well as cookies and raspberry juice. We grew our own berries, so the juice was homemade. The motion of the train was so nice. Looking out the window, I could see the snow-covered land as we traveled. An older man across from me started to snore, which reminded me of my father and made me smile.

My mother had given me an empty calendar book so that I could make notes about my travels. It was then that I started writing about my feelings as I traveled to Paris. I was all by myself, and it felt so right!

A few hours later, I was eating my lunch and found an envelope in my purse from my mother. It contained a very long letter with a poem she had written for me. I read the poem, which she had titled "The Traveler," and I loved it. Mom also enclosed a picture of my whole family, including our dog Telly. She had written down the names of my new family, their address, and their phone number: Mme. and Mr. Jacques Marin, 15 Rue Des Paris, Meudon Val Fleury.

There was another envelope from my dad. He had written a short note and included ten aerograms so I would not forget to write. He had also enclosed some French money, for emergencies.

The train stopped quite often. At eight thirty in the morning, we arrived on time at Gare de L'est. I put on my winter coat and my pretty scarf. Now I had to get that bag down from the overhead compartment. Thanks to two young men, the suitcase was retrieved. However, getting it off the train was another problem. I put a belt around it, expecting it to break open at any time. As I was pushing and pulling the suitcase, some other nice people helped me get it off the train. I said, "Merci beaucoup!" I looked around and saw a man and a lady holding a sign that said, "Marin pour Heidi." Oh boy, I was happy to see them! I waved at them and walked toward them without my luggage. They gave me a big hug.

After looking at my big suitcase, they called a porter to transfer the bag to their car. Right then and there, I made up my mind: from now on, I would always travel light! To this day, I always travel with just a small suitcase. I learned that lesson on my way to Paris!

The ride to Meudon was very nice, and driving through Paris for the first time was magical, a dream come true! It was such a big city, so different from home. I held my umbrella in my hand as if it was a weapon, in case I had to defend myself.

When we got to the apartment building, I thanked God there was an elevator! We rang the apartment doorbell, and two little girls and the maid opened the door. The maid said, "Heidi, this is Valerie and Helen."

The girls looked at me with their big eyes and said, "Bonjour, Heidi." The girls then showed me to my room. It was a small room right next to the theirs. I had a small dresser and a little closet. There wasn't much space for all my things. The bathroom, which I would share with the girls, was across the hall. But my spirits lifted when I realized I had a small balcony off my room—it was great! In the distance there was the Eiffel Tower in all her beauty!

I opened my suitcase and gave Valerie and Helen little presents I had brought from Austria. I had made the gifts, two little teddy bears with matching outfits, with my mother's help. They thanked me, and then we had breakfast. Mr. Marin had to go to work, so it was just Madame, the girls, and me. I had my first croissant and loved it. I still love them!

Because I had not learned the French language yet, we communicated with a lot of hand signals. But that would soon change! One of my responsibilities was to go to the grocery store. I was given a list of things to buy, and Madame went with me to the grocery store, the butcher, and the bakery. Everybody was so nice. I promised everyone that I would learn French as fast as I could.

Another part of my job was to prepare breakfast for the girls and help them get dressed for school, always reminding them to brush their teeth and so on. I would then take them to school, Valerie to kindergarten and Helen to first grade. Their classes were in the same building, maybe a ten-minute walk each way from the apartment. After dropping them off at school, I did grocery shopping, then helped prepare lunch. When I was finished, I returned to the school and brought the girls home for lunch. Valerie attended school only in the morning, but Helen returned to school for the afternoon class. I traveled to my own school by train. I had to take a train two stops and then, using the same ticket, travel on to the Metro subway.

I had my daily work routine as well as homework from my classes. After about two months, I had learned enough French to do the shopping as well as communicate with the other young women at school. They helped me a lot. What also helped me was watching television at night.

Before arriving, I had not known that Jacques Marin, Valerie and Helen's father, was an actor. He was on stage at the Comedie Francaise in the winter, and sometimes I was allowed to see one of his plays. It was fabulous! Just great! He also did some movies, and I was allowed to see some of them. His appearance was typically French. He wasn't very tall, he had a mustache, and he wore a black beret.

I received letters from home. In one letter my mother discussed sending me my violin. I wrote back and told her I could not practice in the apartment, and that was the end of my violin career!

I continued to have a problem with my big suitcase. I kept it under my bed and kept most of my things in it. It was close living, but I wasn't in my room for many hours of the day.

I met other girls who were au pairs for different families. We got together on Sundays. I saved as much money as I could to do special things with my friends.

Two of us went to see Edith Piaf's last performance at the Lido. What a special evening that was. We went for a drink after the show. Some men offered us chocolate candy. I didn't take any, but my friend did. Not long after she ate the candy, she didn't feel well. She was leaning toward me, and I knew we had to get out of there. The guys wanted to help me, but I said no. I had just enough money to take my friend home in a taxi. I dropped her off, and her family drove me home. This could have been a disaster; we never knew what the men were planning. It was very frightening. I learned another valuable lesson: don't eat anything a stranger gives to you.

But that didn't deter us from enjoying the city! We also got tickets to see Josephine Baker at her last performance. I loved the theater and the arts, but the big thing for me was still fashion. I went to the Gallery Lafayette and looked at everything. We also window-shopped at all the big fashion houses: Christian Dior, Chanel, Yves Saint Laurent, and others.

I always liked to sketch and design dresses for myself. I bought some quality fabric, made patterns, and very carefully sewed the dresses by hand.

Madame was impressed when I showed her a finished product. Madame had a very good seamstress who made some beautiful clothes for her. I did not have the advantage of a sewing machine, so I had no choice but to sew everything by hand.

We went to the Louvre every weekend and sometimes to the opera, but my dream was to go to the Ritz Hotel for a coffee and a croissant. I got to know a lady who worked in a boutique in the Tuileries. We brought clothes to her shop before our visits to the hotel, and she allowed us to change in her store. This is how we got ready for our coffee and croissants at the Ritz!

We met some very interesting people at the Ritz. I kept all of their names and all of their information in my address book. After a few trips to the Ritz, the waiter got to know us, and when we arrived, he would say, "Will you have the usual, ladies?"

We'd reply, "Qui c'est parfait!"

After being in Paris for over a year, I decided to take a trip back to Salzburg so I could be home for Christmas. I took the huge suitcase and all my belongings with me. When I returned to Paris, I would be traveling much lighter! I couldn't help but think as I was traveling home, *Here I am, an Austrian girl, traveling through the country, speaking German with a French accent.* Everyone I encountered thought it was so charming.

The trip to Salzburg was wonderful, but I was anxious to get back to Paris and to school. Life in Paris was good! In fact, I was beginning to get very comfortable in my new situation. I even did radio interviews relating to my work as an au pair in Paris! Another new experience was the new, small suitcase that I bought while in Austria. On this trip back to Paris, the suitcase was almost empty since I took very few things—articles of clothing, personal items, some new fabric, face cream, and the like.

In Salzburg, I was a member of the Austrian American Society. Close to my school in Paris, there was an American club. I went there with my Austrian American Society membership card and asked if I could use

Sojourn with Heidi

the club. The desk attendant told me the club was for Americans only. I told him I only wanted to use the pool. The nice gentleman left his desk for a minute and came back with a pamphlet that said, "Welcome to the American Students and Artists Center." He told me I could swim in the pool but to always bring the folder with me. This started another chapter in my life. Boy, did I enjoy that club. It also had an Automat. I would put in some money, and out would come a Butterfinger chocolate. I again thought I had died and gone to heaven! It brought back wonderful memories of my love for Butterfingers.

Because Jacques Marin was a movie actor, he frequently traveled throughout France. He would often take his family—and me—with him. When he acted in a movie that was filmed in a castle, called *Le Chateau code Feodal Josselin*, he rented a house for the duration of the filming. It was an old house with the name Lofi, in a town called St. Quay Portrieux. There was a beach with sculptures carved into the rocks, Côte d'émeraude Rotheneuf. I had never seen anything so magnificent! From there we drove to Le Mont St. Michel. I have included pictures for you to see. The islands have a special allure.

My major means of transportation while there was a bicycle. I used it when doing all the shopping at the small nearby markets. It was such a beautiful place, with farms all around. We also found a little pond where we could go swimming. I spent part of my time finishing up a new dress for myself.

On May 11, 1961, Valerie was having her fifth birthday, so I baked a cake for her. After the birthday celebration, we drove back to Paris.

I was in Paris the day President Kennedy arrived, accompanied by his beautiful wife Jacqueline. We saw his motorcade travel down the Champs Elysees.

The family planned another trip, this time to the South of France, where Jacques Marin was filming another movie. Following the same route as Napoleon, we traveled a full week before arriving at our destination. We stopped at Laffrey and stayed at a beautiful hotel in the town. We visited the statue of Napoleon. We rode through Thand and on to Auxerre, Avallon, Macon, and Lyon. Then we traveled through the Des Gaules tunnel and on to Grenoble and Entrevaux to visit a beautiful castle.

What an adventure for me. We went on to Nice, to the promenade Des

Anglais. I loved seeing the ocean. We covered so much territory and saw so many wonderful cities and regions. We went to Monaco, Monte Carlo, and Menton. We traveled four hundred kilometers around the mountains. I fell in love with every part of it. I was always with my little girls.

Jacques Marin was also filming at the border of Spain, in the Corbieres area. We stayed in a quaint hotel at the bottom of a mountain. I walked up that hill every day because the view was so great. The girls and I had the opportunity to meet Brigitte Bardot, who was also in the movie.

Most of our time was spent in Manton, very close to the Italian border. Every day we went to the beach. The girls loved to swim in the ocean. Swimming was a little difficult because there were no sandy beaches. We had to walk over rocks, and there was a lot of tar on the rocks. All our clothes and towels were stained by the tar.

I had a day off and decided to take the bus to Monte Carlo. I walked around all day long and finally decided to go to a casino. I asked if I could see the casino and was told that I could buy a ticket for the balcony and watch people. It was so great to see women dressed up in long gowns and men in black suits and white shirts—all very formal attire.

I couldn't get enough of it. I was so excited. It was afternoon, and everybody was smoking, and waitresses were walking around with cocktails for everyone. I thought it strange that the casino had no windows, so you had no idea as to the time of day. When I got back outside, the sun was shining, and I thought I had just come back from another world.

Next to the casino was an open-air movie theater, lined with palm trees on both sides, something else I had never seen before. The movie *Orfeu Negro* by Anthony Carlos was playing. I had to see it. It was about Rio de Janeiro at Carnival time. The music and the dancing were so great, and it was even more enchanting in an open-air theater. You were given a seat assignment, then someone would help you to your seat. We had to wait for it to get dark before the movie could start. When the movie ended, I found myself dancing all by myself. This was when I realized that I had missed the last bus home to Manton. I think it was about ten kilometers to get back to the house. Yes, I did have to walk back!

The serpentine road along the ocean at night seemed to never end. I walked as fast as I could. Several cars stopped to give me a ride, but I said no. I had been taught never to go into a stranger's car. I just kept walking.

Finally, after a long time, I got home. When I turned my key in the lock and opened the door, I found Madame and Monsieur waiting for me. I was so sorry for what had happened. I told them the whole story. They gave me a big hug. They had been worried and were just relieved to know that nothing serious had happened to me. I went to bed thinking, *I will never again put myself in a position where I miss the last bus home!*

Of course, we now have cell phones, but even if I'd had a phone, I still would not have had a phone number or address for the apartment. Another lesson from Paris: always have a phone number to call, and always have the address of your temporary residence.

After Manton, we drove back to Paris. We had visited the beach almost every day, so we all had great tans. Life just kept getting better and better! I was having a wonderful time.

I finished school at the Alliance Francaise and then decided to take a course in French literature at the Sorbonne.

In August Madame told me we would be going to England to visit her parents in Leicester. Mr. Marin was filming in another country, so he would not be joining us. Before we left for the trip, my brother Manfred came to Paris for a few days.

He stayed in a little pension not far from the apartment. We had only three days, so I tried to show him as much of the area as possible. We had a great time. We went to the Louvre and other museums and spent one day in Versailles. Before he left on the train for home, he admitted that he was homesick and was anxious to get back to Salzburg. After only three days, how could he be homesick?

My brother was gone, and I was ready for a new adventure. I packed everything I owned into my new small suitcase. A few days later, we drove the car onto a ferry boat and arrived in England later that same day. We were hoping to find a hotel in London. Finally, at 3:00 a.m. we found a place to stay. We were exhausted, so we slept in and had a late breakfast in the morning. English breakfast consisted of tea and toast, nothing like in France!

Before going to Leicester to see Madame's parents, we decided to relocate to a hotel near the beach for one extra night. We visited other family friends, and the girls were with us, of course. Everyone was so nice and welcoming. Since my English wasn't very good, I smiled a lot.

It was the end of August, and the weather was great. In only a few days I would be celebrating my twenty-first birthday! We had a high tea invitation, with cake and chocolate. The cake had twenty-one candles. I had to make a wish and then blow out all the candles. It was all so good but just too much! In addition to the cake, I received many little wrapped parcels. My gifts included bath salts, face cream, some perfume that I loved, and a beautiful bouquet of flowers from the garden. It was such a lovely day. My birthday was like a wonderful dream!

My mother had sent a small parcel to Paris that I hadn't opened. I opened it that night in my room. There was a letter from my mother and one from my father. My mother had sent me some Austrian fabric, which I loved. My father had sent me a little box with a coin in it. In his letter he told me to hang on to the coin and that it might be very valuable one day. It had been given to him from a client who was unable to pay him for services. As of this day, I still have the coin.

The family had a married male friend who visited often. I asked, "Why is he here all the time? He has three children and a very nice wife."

Madame said, "Maybe he wants to see you."

Well, that did it. The next time he came around, I asked him if he had lost something. No, he told me, he hadn't. He said he just liked to look at me.

"Does your wife know what you are doing?" I said in my very bad English.

He answered, "What about my wife?"

I told him to go home and look at his own wife and leave me alone. He never showed up again. Another lesson learned!

Then we went on a trip to Greenhill in Weymouth. We stayed in the Grand Hotel right on the ocean. What a beautiful time we had there. The beach had the most beautiful sand. What a difference from the South of France. We stayed there for about a week. It was a beautiful sunny week.

While we were staying in Leicester, I planned a train trip to Cambridge. I was remembering one day at the Ritz in Paris when I had met a very nice English family. I had liked them very much and corresponded with them when I got to England. The family name was Crick, but that meant nothing to me. My school friend from Salzburg was taking over my job with Madame. I thought I'd like to contact the Crick family and spend time in England.

On September 15, 1961, I found myself taking a train to Cambridge. The children and Madame took me to the train station to see me off.

Jaque Marim and Madame, children Helene and Valerie, 1958.

Heidi Leitner Fearon

Jaque Marim and Madame, children Helene and Valerie, 1958.

5

A New Adventure in Cambridge, England

After many stops and one change to another train, I arrived safely in Cambridge. The address was 19 Portugal Place. Mrs. Crick greeted me at the door and was very happy to see me. After I freshened up, Mrs. Crick wanted to show me Cambridge. It was a university town with so much charm and beautiful old buildings. I was awestruck!

I had a lovely dinner with Mr. Crick and some of their friends. I slept like a baby that night.

The next morning, we had a lovely breakfast, and Mrs. Crick said she'd like to talk with me on the patio before I went back to Leicester. She told me she had a very nice German girl looking after her two girls, but she really needed someone to help cook and entertain. She understood that my main purpose in coming to England was to learn to speak English. If I decided to work for her, she said my school would be just a short walk from their home. "You'd be able to go to school every afternoon," she said.

I told her I had learned to cook in school in Salzburg and could easily do the cooking, no problems with that.

"I am so glad to hear that," she replied. "You can start whenever you can get here."

I was so happy when I boarded the train back to Leicester. On the train I made some notes and wrote a letter to my mom. I asked her to send my school cookbook to my new address: 19 Portugal Place, Cambridge, England.

My mother replied as quickly as she could. She reminded me that I had a job waiting for me in Salzburg and also that my boyfriend was waiting for me. He had been writing the most beautiful letters to me, and I answered them all. I did miss him, but being so busy, I didn't have time to think about anyone else. Then my mom asked me how long I planned to stay in England. I responded to my mother by letter. I was afraid that if I called, my father might answer, and that would not go well.

In my letter I told Mom I wasn't sure how long I would stay in England. But I knew I wanted to learn to speak English. I told her I would go to school every afternoon and help Mrs. Crick with breakfast and dinner. I asked her to please explain everything to Dad. I signed the letter, "Lots of hugs and love, your Heidi."

Now the big day arrived, and my French family dropped me off in Cambridge. We all cried and hugged each other, and I promised to write. My friend from Salzburg had agreed to take my job in Paris, so everything was settled!

The Crick family was waiting for me. They greeted me warmly and showed me to my room, and then we all had lunch together. I got to know the two girls, their au pair (Elenore, the girl from Germany), and Mr. and Mrs. Crick—Francis and Odile. Elenore and I had many conversations in German, our native language. Speaking with her made me feel so happy. Additionally, my room was right next to the kitchen, and I had my own bathroom!

The house, actually two houses joined together, was called the Double Helix. Over the entrance to the house was a double golden spiral. I thought this must be the Double Helix. But I had absolutely no idea what the term and the spiral referenced.

It didn't take me long to discover that Francis Crick was a scientist. I was about to learn a great deal about Mr. Crick and his research, but right now what was most important was that I follow his instructions. "Do not put any food in the middle drawer of the refrigerator," he told me. "This is where I keep my molecules!"

I could not believe what I saw. I asked Francis lots of questions, and of course, he tried to explain, but everything went right over my head. One thing I did understand was that I should never put any food into the middle drawer, and I never did!

Soon I learned that James Watson, Maurice Wilkins, and Francis Crick had discovered the structure of the molecules that created life—they had discovered DNA. They worked together at Cambridge University's famous Cavendish Laboratory.

Mr. Crick was discovering the mystery of life, and my work was in the Crick kitchen, discovering the best menus for the family! Actually, breakfast in England was more work than dinner. Different teas, different eggs, different awful toasts, with marmalade, lemon curd, et cetera. I thought, *What's wrong with a warm croissant, some raspberry jam, and coffee?* But no, not in England! I soon learned all the tricks of the trade, and breakfast was then a breeze. The two girls, eight-year-old Gabriel and nine-year-old Jacqueline, came to all the meals.

They tried to scare me one day. Unbeknown to me, they placed a frog in my apron pocket. I didn't say anything when I found it, but when they weren't looking, I placed the frog on Gabriel's chair. She screamed, and I looked at her. I said, "I wonder where that came from?" She gave me a dirty look. They came up with other tricks, but I always beat them at their own game. Eventually, they stopped.

My big treat after breakfast was playing squash with Francis. I had never played squash before, but I learned very fast and had a lot of fun. I also got to see my first cricket game while working for the family. Everyone dressed in white, which was kind of neat. My first horse race was also quite an experience. The ladies wore beautiful hats and dresses and yelled after their favorite horses!

Most days I went by bike to a local market to get food for dinner. Odile went with me in the beginning, but then I managed to do it all by myself. In the afternoon I went to school to learn English. I learned English much faster than I had learned French in Paris. I loved learning new languages. When I was very young, I had learned a little English from the American family who lived with us in our house in Salzburg. The English I was learning in Cambridge was the King's English, very different from the English they spoke in the USA. I was told I was learning "proper English"!

A visitor from Australia was staying at the Crick house, and we discovered that she soon would be celebrating her twenty-first birthday. Her name was Jenny, and her birthday was October 28, 1940. She was my age and very nice.

This was the first party I was to organize with Odile. Thanks to my Austrian cookbook, I made the best Sacher torte for Jenny's birthday. We called it a toga party, and everybody draped sheets over themselves, trying to represent different Greek characters. We all had fun.

The weeks went by very fast. I was becoming quite proficient in English. I met a lot of nice boys. We all loved dancing at a local jazz club. Christmas came, and soon it was 1962.

What a year, 1962. This was the year when Francis Crick, James Watson, and Maurice Wilkins won the Nobel Prize. Of course, a great party celebrating the event was a *must*! I have never seen so much champagne consumed. The party was catered, but I helped with organizing, preparing, and participating. I made myself a new outfit for the occasion.

At the big champagne party for the Nobel Prize winners, I met some interesting scientists from the United States and a very nice lawyer from Boston. The lawyer asked me if I had ever been to the United States. I said no, I hadn't. He told me he had three children, and his wife was looking for someone to care for them—someone who could offer a European influence. I thought, *Here is another possible wonderful opportunity!* I said I had to think about it. However, I knew America would be great! Later, you will learn how this man and his family become part of my life.

Crick, Watson, and Wilkins received 50,000 pounds as part of the Nobel Prize. The information was on the news and in all the newspapers. I learned so much about these impressive men from reading the articles.

The day after the party, Francis gave Eleanor and me twenty pounds each. I hopped around like a wild animal and thanked Francis for being so generous. Now I had enough money to fly back to Austria.

It was inevitable that I would have to go back to Austria. After all, I had graduated English school and was quite good at speaking "proper" English.

Before it came time to leave, there were other parties. One in particular stayed in my mind. Odile was an artist and painter. She made the invitation and included a drawing of a nude girl on it. We had the invitations printed and sent them out. I still have the original invitation. It read:

> Francis and Odile Crick
> Invite you to a STUDIO PARTY
> At The Golden Helix
> 19 Portugal Place

Friday, First of June 1962, at 9 pm.
Dress: Artists, Models or Dancing Girls

Well, what a party that was! They hired a nude model to pose so guests could sketch her. She draped herself on a leopard skin on a small couch. There was a rope in front of her with some tassels attached. In front of the area was a small sign which read, "DO NOT TOUCH."

I was assigned the task of handing each guest a sketch pad and a black charcoal pen. Everybody was asked to sketch the model. People were lining up to see her. I have to say she had a superb body. There must have been about seventy or eighty people in attendance.

There was a full bar with a bartender, a great buffet with a lot of food, and a fruit and dessert table. The food was outstanding, and everyone had a wonderful time. The guests consumed ample amounts of alcohol, which was definitely reflected in their sketches. The next day I collected many of the sketches, and we looked at them during breakfast. I laughed so much! What fun!

Crisk daughters in England namely Gabrielle and Jacqueline, 1961.

Heidi Leitner Fearon

NOBELISTS IN WAITING: Crick, left, and Watson have coffee at the Cavendish laboratory after their paper appeared in *Nature*

Francis Crisk and Watson winning the Nobel Prize for discovering DNA.

Francis and Odile Crick

invite you to

A STUDIO PARTY

at

The Golden Helix
19 Portugal Place
on Friday, 1st June 1962 at 9. p.m.

Dress : Artists, Models or Dancing Girls

R.S.V.P.

Studio Party Invitation, 1962.

6

Back to Salzburg but for How Long?

Well, in August I packed my smaller suitcase again and got ready to fly home to Salzburg, Austria. I still cannot believe that God gave me the chance to live with the Crick family. I learned so much. They encouraged me to never change and wished me every happiness with my future. We said our goodbyes and hugged each other. Then a friend drove me to the train station. At first I had planned on flying home, but after careful thought I had realized the flight would use up all my savings. The long train ride would give me time to prepare to see my parents, my boyfriend, and my waiting job.

When I arrived in Salzburg, my family and many friends were there to greet me, including my boyfriend. He was happy I was home.

I unpacked and gave my family some gifts from England. I had so many stories to tell. Then I went to Lanz of Salzburg to let them know I was back and ready to start work if they needed me.

I loved walking around my home city in my Austrian dirndl. The tourists would take photos of me and ask me questions, and I could answer them in English. One gentleman who asked me some questions was from New York. Experience had taught me to take advantage of the moment, so I continued my practice of writing names and information in my address book. I wrote down the gentleman's name and address and phone number, thinking, *Well, you never know!* We had coffee together at the Café Tomaselli, and I learned he was a professor at New York University. His name was Ernest van den Haag, a published American Dutch sociologist.

Everything was almost back to normal when my father's secretary, Herr Seneternick, called me in from the garden and gave me some mail. I always liked receiving mail, and I still do.

I opened the big envelope from America, and boy, I couldn't believe what I saw.

No, no, it can't be, I thought. I slowly walked back to the garden, where my mom was sitting in the sun, and sat down beside her.

"Okay, Heidi, what's up? You are not saying anything. Are you getting married or something?"

"No, no, Mom. I am going to Butterfinger country."

"You are doing what?"

"I am going to America."

"No, Heidi, you are not," she said.

"Look, I got a ticket to Boston in the mail!"

"Oh my God," my mother said. She looked at me and started to cry, and I cried too! "What about your job and your boyfriend and us?" Mom said.

I told her I'd return immediately if I didn't like it. I'd come right back!

Now here I went again. I had to tell everyone about the new plan, including my father. After I told him my news, he just said, "I am not surprised anymore. All I can say is I hope all goes well and make me proud of you."

My flight was in three weeks. The ticket was with Icelandic Airlines (Loftleidia), and my flight left from Luxembourg. Somehow I had to get to Luxembourg. A friend of my brother said he had a car and would drive me there. His name was Rudi, and I'd known him for many years. He had attended the same school as my brother.

My parents invited all of my friends to a goodbye party. Rudi was also there, and he explained to everyone how he was going to drive me to Luxembourg. The next day, there were more hugs and goodbyes, and we were off.

The drive to Munich would take about two hours. We gassed up and drove away. Mom had made sandwiches for the trip and packed some drinks. All of a sudden, the car made a terrible noise, and then it stopped! Oh my God, how was I going to get to the airport? We had to be towed to a repair shop, and they told us it would take two days to get the part, and then they could fix it. Rudi did not have enough money for the repair and had to ask his father to bail him out.

Now I had to travel by train. I bought my ticket and went via Koblenz to Luxembourg. I met some very nice people on the train. They were from Paris, and I was happy to speak French again.

I then traveled by bus to the airport. I went to my gate, got my seat assignment, checked my luggage, and realized I had four more hours before the plane would depart. I bought an aerogram and started to write my parents a long letter about everything that had happened. Since this was my first flight, I thought I had to dress beautifully. I was wearing a lovely suit and high heels. I even had a matching hat. Boy, did all that change—now we travel in comfortable clothes and shoes!

On the flight I got to know a German girl and two other young girls flying with her. Finally, at 6:50 p.m. we were able to board the plane. I had a very nice window seat and couldn't get enough of all the excitement. I didn't even notice that a very nice lady had taken her seat next to me. When the plane took off and cut through the clouds, the whole sky turned red and orange. The sun was setting over the ocean, and it was so beautiful. The stewardess was very nice and helped me put my table down for dinner. This was all so new to me. I also got a small bottle of wine, and I enjoyed everything to the fullest. I had a nap, and then the captain announced that we had to fasten our seatbelts because we were about to land in Reykjavik.

It was freezing cold, and we had to walk down the plane's steps to the bus. By that time I couldn't stand wearing the high heels anymore, but they were all I had. We all got something to eat. We were later told to reboard the plane; our next landing would be Garner, Newfoundland.

The final flight was smooth and relaxing. We flew over Canada, and the captain announced, "We have now reached the American continent." Tears came running down my cheeks. I was approaching the Butterfinger country.

7

America, Here I Come

We landed in New York, and a lady met me with a message and another plane ticket. The message had the name of my new family and their telephone number. It also said, "Heidi, welcome to the United States of America."

The lady said we had to go fast because the plane to Boston was leaving in thirty minutes. I had just gotten to my seat when the engine started. I was so excited that my stomach was unsettled. I could not quite digest all of this. I finally relaxed and was feeling better when I heard the captain announce that we were about to land. I was very excited and thought I would gladly do this all over again, but not wearing high heels!

We arrived in Boston, and the plane landed. I got off slowly with my hand luggage in one hand and my passport close by. I had to fill out a customs declaration, which I put into my passport. I also had a letter from my new Boston family confirming my visit and saying that they were also my sponsors.

Going through customs and finding the right carousel for my luggage was a long process. I waited and waited, but yes, my smaller bag did make it! While looking for the exit sign, I decided I had to make one more stop to the bathroom. As I exited the airport, I took a deep breath. When the sliding doors opened, I realized a new phase of my life was about to begin! Hello, Boston!

I looked around to see if anyone was holding a card with my name. Finally, I saw the gentleman I had met in England, standing with his wife. My name was on a piece of paper, and I was so happy to see them.

"Heidi, it is so nice to see you again," he said. We hugged, and I got to meet Shirley, his wife. Everything was so different, including the English. This was not proper English, but it sounded friendly, and I could understand everything. My first time in a new country, and I didn't have to learn a new language—what a relief!

We walked to the parking lot and climbed into a dream car. It was the nicest car I'd ever seen. We drove to 1 Pelham Road in Lexington Heights.

Entering the wonderful house was another experience. The children, Marsha, Larry, and Beverly, were lined up to greet me. And Toppy, their very nice dog, sat on the steps with his tail wagging. As I tried to pet the dog, he gave me a kiss on the nose. My very first kiss in the United States of America! The family showed me to my room, and I felt at home immediately!

The first day, I slept in, but Mr. and Mrs. Rich had to drive to the hospital to visit Shirley's grandmother, who was not well. But the welcoming feeling continued when I received a phone call from Mr. Rich's secretary. She wanted to welcome me to the United States.

The children—Marsha, twelve; Larry, fourteen; and Beverly, nine—were so nice to me. We had a lot of fun together. I had my Austrian cookbook with me and showed them a lot of new things to cook. They all liked my pastries. I did not want to gain weight, so I had to watch what I ate.

This wonderful family essentially adopted me as their fourth child! I really had nothing in particular to do. "Heidi, do whatever you want," they said. "We are just happy that you are here." I could play records and watch TV, for example. Larry had a photo lab, and he tried to teach me how to develop my own pictures.

I also went to the local university to sign up for some courses. I was interested in learning to type in English and also in learning English shorthand. The school asked me if I would do a volunteer job and gave me a list of different choices. One of the options was to volunteer as a ballroom dance instructor. I said yes, I would do it if I had a good leader!

Bill Yang was the dance instructor, and he was looking for someone to work with him. I was told he could meet with me the next day if I had time. "Oh yes," I said, "I'll be there!" Mrs. Rich told me the family had an extra car I could use. This would be a fine way to get to school and the studio, and I was very appreciative. However, there was one problem: I didn't know how to drive!

I went to meet Bill the dance instructor, who was a tall, slim Asian man. He shook my hand and said, "Let's try a dance." We danced like we had danced together for years. "One more dance?" he asked. "I love the quickstep—can you do that one?"

"You lead me, and I will follow you," I said.

He told me I was the third person he had tried to dance with, and I was the best one.

Before I left, I asked him a question. "Do you know how to drive a car?"

He said he did. I asked, "If I dance with you, can you teach me how to drive a car?"

"Okay, I will do that."

I was so happy that day as I ran to the bus stop and went home.

When I arrived home, I found a big box in my closet. I asked Shirley about it. She told me it was a sewing machine from her mother, but it had never been used. I could hardly speak. I asked very timidly if I could use it.

"Of course, you can, if you can make it work!"

I thanked her and thanked her. I told her I could figure it out. What a great day that was!

Well, it took me some time to figure it out. The machine was very heavy, but I managed to lift it. It was an electric sewing machine, and it fit nicely on my desk. I found an electrical plug, plugged it in, and also discovered how to insert the foot! After I completed the assembly of the equipment, I found a small pamphlet of instructions. I followed the directions and could now thread the machine and slide the bobbin into the lower bobbin holder. Now for the test! There was a small piece of fabric under the needle, and off I went. It worked! I learned how to make longer stitches and also how to go zigzag on the machine. My whole life had changed. I had a sewing machine, oh my God!

The next day, I walked to a small fabric store and bought fabric to make a blouse. The fabric was yellow and white squares. After everyone went to bed, I used an old newspaper to make the pattern for my new blouse. The next afternoon, I started my project. The girls came into my room and asked what I was doing. I told them I was making a blouse. They

Sojourn with Heidi

wanted to learn how to do it. They had never seen a sewing machine and didn't know how one worked.

I explained the whole procedure and told them it would be possible for us to make anything. I knew how to sew. Right away, Marsha asked if she could make a poodle skirt. I said of course and that I'd teach her how to use the machine.

Beverly just looked at me, then fetched her mom. "Mom, do you know what Heidi can do? Come and see."

Now we were all together in my room, looking at the sewing machine. I said to Mrs. Rich, "All we need is fabric and some paper for patterns. Then I can make anything."

My life changed after I told them I could make patterns for all the clothes they liked. I also told them their clothes would be originals, "designed by Heidi"—no one else could ever have the same clothes. They loved this even more.

I made that poodle skirt, and after that I was sewing all the time. Both girls were eager to learn and quick to improve their skills. Their first project was a potholder for their mom's birthday.

When I was in Paris, my girlfriend from Salzburg was also there. I learned that she now wanted to come to America. I went to my neighbors, the Alberts, and asked them if they needed an au pair, like they had when we were in Paris. Mrs. Alberts told me she had to speak with her husband and also the children. She'd let me know soon. My good luck was with me again. They agreed to let my friend come. I sent her an express letter with the good news and the names and ages of the children. Edda would arrive in about four weeks.

This gave me just enough time to learn how to drive the Plymouth, with the shift on the wheel. I recruited Bill, and off we went. He was very patient with me. He knew how much I wanted to learn how to drive.

There was a convent on top of a hill in town. It had a large parking lot that was perfect for lessons. Bill drove the car to the lot, where I had my first driving lesson. I worked hard and did my best to be a good student. I also asked Mrs. Rich if the car could be left at the convent so I could continue to practice driving the car. She agreed.

I learned how to drive that car and one day ventured down the hill all by myself.

Then I drove it back up the hill and parked it at the convent. I was working very hard at becoming a capable driver in as short a period as possible. All this time, I was driving the family car. On the day my friend Edda was arriving from Salzburg, Mrs. Albert, her two children, and I went to the airport to meet her, and I drove the car!

One thing I enjoyed was walking the Riches' family dog in the afternoon, and often I'd take Mrs. Alberts's dog with me. They were very compatible. I took them through the woods to a spot that was very special to me.

Once when visiting this secret location, I wrote this poem:

My Hidden Spot

How hidden can I be,
alone and just for me.
Look at the grass
and up a tree.
Can hardly believe
that all this can be.

An ant is walking over my arm,
it tickles me but doesn't do harm.
The wind so soft,
and the grass high and fine.
I feel in my heart
this world is all mine!

Can I really dream with open eyes?
Things come to me more like a surprise,
but if I see a boat with a sail,
it seems to me like a fairy tale.
So I turn around on my hidden spot
and start walking home—yes, I almost forgot!

Then with my two dogs on leashes, I'd walk back home. My life was getting more hectic, but I loved every moment of it.

The family went on many trips. Springfield was one trip; Sturbridge

Village was another outing. I met a new friend through the Rich family, named Adam. He owned a private plane, and one day we flew to Provincetown. What a treat that was!

I went to New York City on several occasions. Professor Ernest van den Haag, whom I had met in Salzburg, had started to correspond with me and invited me to see New York. We double-dated several times with William F. Buckley. The two had written a book together. I had a wonderful time seeing the Cloisters and the Empire State Building as well as other exciting New York attractions.

One day when visiting New York, I met my girlfriend Christl, who was also from Salzburg. She worked at Sig and Buchmeier as a salesperson. They sold Austrian clothing in that store, including Lanz from Salzburg.

Back in Boston, the family invited me to go to a party. It was a sales party to sell office space in a new building. I was sitting in a corner, enjoying a glass of wine, when this nice salesman approached me. He wanted to know why I was at the party.

I told him I was with the Rich family. During our conversation, I mentioned my interest in seeing Canada, and he told me he was from Montreal. He gave me his business card; his name was Gary Hewson. He told me he had a very good friend who lived in Montreal who was single and worked for *Time* magazine. His name was Fred Kirkwood. Gary thought we should meet. Of course, at that time I didn't know where life would take me, so I added his name and number into my address book. You never know!

I met a new girlfriend from Montreal who was taking dance lessons at the studio.

She told me that if I went to Montreal, her parents would have a room for me there. Everything was going around in my head. Yes, I really wanted to go to Montreal! There was only one problem: I wanted to drive, and although I had learned how to drive with Bill, I did not have an official driver's license.

I drove myself to the Department of Motor Vehicles so I could get a book to study for the test. Every night, I studied my driving book, and after two weeks, I had enough nerve to drive myself to the location where I would take the driving test. This happened to be three days before my twenty-third birthday.

I passed the test! I had to park the car on a hill, then back up into a space between two cars—not a problem for me. I knew how to drive; I had been driving without a license for a long time now. In the process of getting my driver's license, I also had to be photographed for the license. Everyone congratulated me for doing such a great job. Then the man who had given me the test asked how I was getting home. I had to think quickly! I said someone had driven me to the office and was also taking me home.

I was so happy when I had that license in my hand. By the way, this was the only test I'd ever taken in my whole life. I still can't believe it.

8

Road Trip to Montreal

It was now the second day of October 1963, and I was twenty-three years old and driving to Canada! My Montreal girlfriend's parents had agreed that I could stay with them. So I had a place to stay. Adam, who drove me, planned to find a hotel room for himself.

What a difference when you can legally drive a car. I was very lucky that nothing ever happened to me. I originally had been too shy to tell my family that I could not drive a car. As Frank Sinatra would say, I did it my way, although I would not recommend this to anyone. I was one very lucky girl!

Now that I had my driving license, I asked Adam if I could drive across the border into Canada. He said yes, and I did! However, by the time we crossed the border, we were so tired. We pulled off the highway to find a quiet spot to sleep for a few hours. Once we were refreshed, we looked for a restaurant to have some breakfast. I loved that everyone spoke French. I noticed that the French here was very different from the French I had learned in Paris, but I was able to understand everything. After eating, we drove around Montreal to find my friend's house in Outremont. We had a map of the city and finally found the right house.

The family was waiting for me and greeted me with open arms. We were invited to come inside the house. I took my small suitcase and handbag with me, traveling light as usual. The family was so nice. We all spoke French, and poor Adam did not understand a word of it. I asked the family if they knew of a hotel for Adam. His plan was to stay for about three days, then drive back to Boston.

During the next three days, we did as much sightseeing as we could, driving all around Montreal. I loved the city right away. We walked up to Mount Royal and loved the view of the city. We saw the Saint Lawrence River in the distance. The weather was perfect. Then Adam had to leave and drive back to Boston. Now I was alone and exhausted.

After two days I found the card with the telephone number of the man who worked for *Time* magazine, Fred Kirkwood. I called him, and he suggested that he take me to dinner. I said yes, maybe tomorrow, and gave him my address.

Then he suggested that I take a bus and meet him at a little Swiss restaurant he thought I might like. I asked him if he had a car.

"Yes, I have a car, but I would have to go home to get it," he said.

I responded, "Well, nice talking with you, but I don't take a bus for a first date," and I hung up the phone.

Two days later, Fred called me back. He said that if I agreed to have dinner with him, he would come by for me in his car. That sounded much better! I said okay. I gave him my address again, and I was ready to be picked up at 6:30 p.m.

He arrived driving a big Studebaker convertible. He rang the doorbell, and I opened the door. He was very funny and made amusing comments about my insistence on his coming to my house and taking me to the restaurant. Dinner was great.

Fred was not very tall or very slim. Actually, he was an average-looking guy but very charming and very funny. He had a miniature poodle he called Charlie Brown. We dated several times more before my Boston family came to bring me back home, and I was intrigued by his humor. Over the course of time, I met some of his friends and family. He was the youngest of eight siblings.

Although Fred was on my mind, I was now back in Boston and planning to visit Salzburg to see my family. But Fred was persistent, calling almost every day. I remember thinking, *I think I'm falling in love with this man.* He asked me if I would marry him. What nerves he had!

But no one at home in Salzburg knew much about Fred. I had mentioned him to my mom in my last letter to her, but that's all.

On the eleventh of November 1963, I flew to Austria. Fred wrote many beautiful letters and wanted me to come to Montreal for his birthday, which happened to be January 1.

I told my parents that I thought I was in love. My dad said, "Why doesn't he come to Salzburg so we can meet the gentleman?" He was anxious to meet Fred, although nothing I did surprised him anymore.

I told my father that I would see Fred on his birthday, and then I would know more. I left Salzburg and went back to Canada for Fred's birthday. During this time I got to know him very well. I decided I would be staying in Canada. My Outremont family helped me find a job as an au pair. I would have my own place.

I applied for a Canadian driver's license so that I could drive the children to their activities. Then I realized that in three months my visa would expire. But love does conquer all. Problem solved—Fred asked me to marry him. We really got along very well. It pleased my father that Fred asked him for my hand in marriage. After that, we got married!

Fred's brother Tom and his wife Diane hosted a beautiful wedding reception for us. Fred bought me a beautiful white Volvo as a wedding gift, and after the reception, we drove off to begin our honeymoon.

Well, we didn't get very far that first night. We just made it to downtown to the Queen Elizabeth Hotel. The next day would be Quebec City. We decided to live it up and went for a horse and buggy ride through the city. I was wearing high heels, and as I was getting out of the buggy, I caught my heel in a crack on the buggy's wooden floor. Fred did not realize my predicament and somehow gave me a push to help me down. As a result, I went headfirst onto the cement ground. The next thing I knew, I had an ice bag on my head. I was lying under a tree and had a big bump on my forehead. Boy, did it hurt!

The hotel physician examined me, gave me some medication, and told me to stay put and keep using the ice. I said to myself, *This must be how they came up with the expression "Not tonight, dear, I have a headache"*!

After a few days, I started to feel better. I was lucky I hadn't broken a leg or an arm or maybe my back. We stopped at another Chateaux hotel, and then we drove back to Montreal.

I had promised my family that Fred and I would come to Salzburg in the summer, and we did. Everyone wanted to meet Fred, especially my parents. My father introduced Fred to some Austrian Schnapps, and they both got Schnuckefied. My parents approved of Fred, and we had a good time with friends and family.

Of course, my goal was to work in the fashion world in some capacity. I had to start somewhere. As luck would have it, back in Montreal I found a job as an assistant patternmaker. I would be located in a basement with no windows and neon lights. The good thing about the job was that I learned how patterns were made in Canada. I learned to think in inches and learned about seam allowance. The work environment may not have been pretty, but I was working in the world of fashion, which made me very happy. I sometimes stayed late at work so that I could check out the work. I quickly learned the patternmaker's job because it was so similar to what I had learned in Austria.

After this apprenticeship, I decided to broaden my horizons. I had a car and was able to travel to different locations in search of a new job. My next job was with a company called Josef, and here two ladies would be making patterns.

I loved to sketch my designs, and my boss liked my work. I soon discovered that I was in store for a new challenge. The boss bought out an Italian company known for making the most beautiful hand-screened scarves. The challenge for me was to design a bikini out of one scarf. Other scarves would be used for the design of cover-ups. We were allowed to use two scarves for a top or a beach sweeper.

I loved the challenge. In no time at all, we were ready to have a fashion show at the 747 restaurant, which was on the top floor of a very fashionable hotel. I sketched all my designs and signed them "HEIDI." This way our clients, most of them from Fifth Avenue in New York City, would know who had done the design.

The funny thing about those beautiful bikinis is that the fabric was so delicate, we had to advertise that the bikinis were non-swimmable! Non-swimmable! How crazy was that? They were pure silk and very beautiful, and we sold every one.

Not too long after the show, I received a call at work from a man who was in the fashion business. He and his assistants wanted to take me to lunch. I explained that I had only one hour for lunch, and they agreed to meet me at a small restaurant across the street from my work. I told them I would meet with them at twelve noon the next day.

The next afternoon, I met a very nice English gentleman and his assistant Diane. They offered me a job working for a company that had a total of thirty-six fashion stores throughout Canada. I would be required to design dresses to go with matching coats. I told them that I had not designed these kinds of items before but would like to try.

Although they did not know my current salary, their offer was double my current earnings. This gave me an extra push to seriously consider the job. I told them I would think about it and call them with an answer within a few days. I was so happy about the offer and wanted to dance all the way home.

Fred's advice was to do whatever I thought was best. I started to think dresses and sketched many for my portfolio. I accepted the new job and gave Josef two weeks' notice.

My new workplace was a longer commute, but I had indoor parking and would be working with some very nice people. I still created most of my own patterns, but now I had an assistant patternmaker helping me. I always had a coat design in front of me, sometimes just a sketch but most of the time the finished product. This job offered me so many more opportunities. I would be in charge of the new designs. Fortunately, I happened to be the first model size and could try the dresses on before I put them into the collection.

This was around the time that computers were being introduced into the workplace. Most of our work was done entirely by hand. I had to create weekly statements for all the stores noting which of my designs were selling. All my tracking and inventory distribution were done manually. Whatever sold in Halifax didn't always sell in Vancouver. I learned very quickly how to design and please clients in all of our Canada locations.

My husband still worked for *Time* magazine. One of his responsibilities this particular year was to organize a large charity event with a Roman theme. The magazine hired an Italian band, catered Italian food, and had big columns installed to create an Italian decor. Everything was Italian. They tried to hire Gina Lollobrigida to add to the Italian flair, but she was filming elsewhere and could not attend. They did, however, find a most suitable fortune teller who would entertain the crowd with her magical insight into the future.

All the women were dressed in long evening gowns, and it was very festive. The room seated five hundred people for dinner. The first thing I did was line up for the fortune teller. She wore a turban on her head, big earrings, and a long colorful skirt, and she had a crystal ball. I waited a long time to see her, but it was finally my turn.

I sat down, and she took my hand. She told me, "Oh my, I see something. Oh, oh."

I asked, "What is it? Is it something good?"

She said, "That depends. You are pregnant, and it is going to be a boy."

I did not tell anyone about her remark, not even my husband. What did an Italian fortune teller know anyway?

At that time I had worked almost one year with D'Allaird. My boss, Mr. Burpee, asked me into his office. This was Christmas time, 1965. He asked me, "What is going on with your dresses? You have little bows at the neck, and some dresses have a yoke with some shirring in the front. Are you pregnant?"

I had to be truthful and tell him yes. I told him I had just gotten the news.

"Well, Heidi, I have an interesting idea if you're willing to do it. Would you like to design your own maternity line?"

I had never given it a thought before this moment. I'd be able to design, model, and market my own maternity line! I could now dress myself for the next nine months. I have to say this was a very easy decision for me. I was the best-dressed pregnant lady in town!

I was consumed by my pregnancy. I didn't drink and never smoked. I did yoga every day and read all the beautiful poems my mom wrote for me. This was also the time I asked my father to come to Montreal for a visit.

My father didn't like to write letters. I promised him that I would reply to each of his letters and would include some Canadian money in with the letters. I wanted him to have some Canadian money, to spend when he arrived. This is the only reason that I have so many beautiful letters from my dad, in his own handwriting.

When he came to Canada, he had all the Canadian dollars I had sent him. But he could never spend any of it because Fred paid for everything. Before Dad went back to Austria, he bought something in yellow for the baby and a gift for my mom.

Those nine months of my pregnancy went by very fast. At that time we did not have sonograms to detect the sex of the baby. Fred wanted a boy so badly. I made the crib all in pink just in case it was a girl. But Fred got his wish.

On July 31, a healthy baby boy was born in Montreal General Hospital. We named him Scott. He was a bundle of joy! This is when I told my husband about the fortune teller's prediction. At that time I hadn't known I was pregnant. And she was right—just amazing!

Fred was the youngest of eight siblings, at the end of the line. For once he had wanted to be number one, so I had made him number one throughout our marriage. But now, with a new baby, someone else would need me more. Fred was now second in line.

After the baby was born, Fred smuggled a rum and Coke into the hospital to surprise me. I hadn't drunk alcohol for nine months, and he thought this was a time to celebrate. I enjoyed the drink, and then I had to breastfeed my new son.

When it was time for the next feeding, the nurse didn't bring me the baby. She told me he was fast asleep and she didn't want to wake him. I thought about the rum and Coke! I was the guilty one because the rum must have had an effect on my breast milk. I learned another lesson: don't drink when you are breastfeeding.

When our first Christmas with our new baby arrived, I had to call my parents and brother to wish them a Merry Christmas. All was well in Austria, and all was well with my new family in Canada.

Six months later, I went to Austria for the first time with my little boy. My parents were so happy with the new addition to the family. My father wanted to show Scott the Untersberg, our highest mountain. We all made the day trip. It was a very happy visit. My brother, who had no children, borrowed Scott and his pram and went for a walk. Later we went swimming in our pool, and Scott loved playing with all the other children.

Fast-forward again, and we were back in Canada for our second Christmas. I called my parents to wish them happy holidays, and my mother answered the phone. At first she was very quiet. I was very happy with Scott sitting on my lap and was telling Mom all my news. Then I asked to speak to Dad. Mom started to cry. She had to tell me that my father had passed away a few days earlier. I was devastated to hear the awful news and wanted to know how Dad had died.

Mom told me, crying all the time, that he had been cooking gulasch, and all of a sudden, he collapsed and passed out. He never woke up. He ruptured his aorta and bled to death. We were both in tears for a very long time. This was the saddest Christmas I can remember.

In the spring I went to Salzburg to stay with my mom for three months. Being with Scottilein was so helpful and comforting for my mother. My mom wore only black while I was there. Seeing her in black all the time made me very sad. When I went back to Canada, I bought Mom a beautiful colorful scarf and sent it to her. I told her Dad would have wanted her to wear colorful things. She wore that scarf often.

My work on my new maternity line kept me very busy because it was doing so well. Because of our success, my boss suggested doing a line of clothes for larger women. I thought, *Why not?* It should be easy—I just make the tops longer and choose some appropriate fabric. I suggested that rather than calling the line extra large, we call it "Extra Lovely." The line sold well, and I was pleased!

I was playing a lot of tennis around this time, so with my boss's support, I launched my own tennis line. We called it Heidi-Ho. I had only ten pieces in the collection, but because we made the clothing in our own factory, we had great quality control, and it sold very well.

I had my little boy with me all the time. Scott developed language skills very early in his life. I spoke with him in German, my husband spoke to him in English, and at age two he went to a French kindergarten. As a very young boy, he mastered three languages.

Around this same time, we bought our first and only house. It was in Montreal West. We were in an English community, and our address was 11 Ballantyne Street.

Once Scott started first grade, I had more time to work. My boss insisted that I take Scott to school and be there when his day at school ended. At that time Scott didn't know I worked.

I looked for a part-time babysitter to help me out and hired Mimi Yang. She was tall and the most lovely person. I told her that I had done ballroom dancing at Boston University with a tall fella named Bill Yang. She told me that was her brother! I said, "You have got to be kidding me, Mimi!" What a small world!

Mimi was great with Scott, and he loved her. She loved Scott so much that later in life, when she got married, she named her son Scott.

Life was moving along nicely. Fred and I joined the Royal St. Lawrence Yacht Club. Fred bought a twenty-five-foot sailboat, and we named her *Heidi-Ho*. Scott learned how to swim in swimming lessons, and he loved the water. When he got to be about nine, we got him his first sailing boat, a little Optimist pram.

Fred and I met another sailing couple at the yacht club named Bob and Sylvia, and we decided to go bareboat chartering together. We had to pass a course to qualify to charter a boat. We passed and decided to charter a boat out of Tortola. Our boat, the *Heidi-Ho*, was out of the water, wrapped with canvas, and covered for the winter. This was the end of January and a great time to get some sun in the Caribbean. We chartered a thirty-nine-foot sloop named *The Crazy 8*.

With Mimi looking after Scott, we left the first week of February to fly to Tortola. The year was 1978. I had found some cute fabric—white, blue, and red, with sailors and sailboats—and had designed matching outfits for the four of us. With the bright sun, I thought it would be wise to cover up for the first few days.

We had packed our small duffel bag for our trip: bathing suits, shorts, and T-shirts were all we needed! We were bundled up leaving Montreal. We had dressed like onions so we could peel off clothes as we headed to the warm weather in the Caribbean.

Tortola was paradise for us. Our first time in a taxi, an open minibus with a driver who sang while rounding the corners at full speed, was scary. We were happy when he dropped us off at the hotel. We had a great dinner accompanied by a magnificent sunset. We went to bed early so we'd be ready for the boat the next morning.

We were at the marina early and were introduced to *The Crazy 8*! We were so excited and anticipating a wonderful sail!

After a briefing about the boat, we went off to buy provisions for the ten-day trip. We finally had everything in place and were ready to take off, pulling a small dinghy. The boys knew how to start the little outboard. The boat had a center cockpit. We had a big stateroom, and Bob and Sylvia slept in the forward cabin, which we called the honeymoon suite.

The galley, dining area, and living quarters were in the center of the boat, and no one slept there.

All went well until the second night. I got up during the night to get a drink of water and couldn't help but notice the beautiful full moon illuminating our boat. As I was sitting down at the table, I felt something warm touching my leg. I screamed. Suddenly, there was a body running away from under the table. He jumped over the side and swam away.

Now everyone was awake. We turned on all the lights to assess the situation.

Boy, were we lucky. We found a black garbage bag packed with all our valuables and even the cassette player belonging to the boat, which had been screwed to the wall—all of these items ready to be stolen. We learned our lesson: watch out for thieves when at anchor.

Another time, while I was at the helm, we were sailing at perfect speed, and I felt like I hit something. It was a big whale coming up in front of the boat! What a scary experience. Jacque Cousteau was filming stories about the whales at the time.

We all had a wonderful time, but it had to come to an end. Back at Tortola, we went to the free marina (free because you could not bring any open liquor bottles back with you). We had everything ready for the trip home and decided to have a goodbye drink for the road. There was a man sitting at the bar drinking. I finally said, "We better go so we don't miss our taxi."

The man sitting at the bar told us not to worry—he was the driver. Then Fred told him we had to catch a small plane to Puerto Rico. The guy again said, "Don't worry. I am also the pilot." Thank God Fred knew how to fly a plane. He would definitely sit in the copilot's seat on this trip!

We made it back to Montreal with Caribbean tans and bundled up for the cold weather. We all had our stories to tell.

9

Now Back to the Real World

Scott was very active in the junior sailing school and did a lot of sailing. He also was very musical and started to learn to play the xylophone with a group of children. He loved sports, especially tennis. We played tennis at Montreal West and at the yacht club. I was a busy mom, driving Scott to all of his activities.

I also registered Scott for karate lessons, but I wanted him to take the bus to Westmount. Initially, I went on the bus with him. It was only four stops, but then he had to cross the street to get to the YMCA. The first time he traveled on the bus by himself, I followed the bus to make sure he crossed the street at the light. All went well.

There was one day when I asked Scott to cut the grass in the backyard. I had one of those push mowers, and I thought he could help us with the lawn. He did it and then gave me a bill for $3.50. I reviewed the bill and gave him the $3.50. When he came to dinner, I served him some chicken with veggies and a nice dessert. Afterward, I asked Scott if he would like another piece of dessert.

"Yes, Mom. This is good!"

Once he had finished, I gave Scott a bill for $4.50.

He said, "Mom, you cannot do that!"

I replied, "Okay, if you don't charge me for cutting the grass, I won't charge you for dinner." We shook hands, and Scott gave me back the $3.50. This was a great teaching opportunity, and it went very well!

Next to his music and sports, Scott loved magic. There was a store near his school where you could buy magic tricks. Many amateur magicians tried their tricks out in the store, and Scott was mesmerized by the tricks. I bought him some easy ones, and boy, did he love that.

The summer of Scott's eleventh birthday, we went to Europe for the summer and traveled to Hamburg to visit my mother's sister Heidi and her husband Kurt. Uncle Kurt wanted to buy Scott a birthday present. All Scott wanted was a new magic trick. We went to a fantastic magic shop in Hamburg, where Scott chose a Samba ball. This was the beginning of Scott becoming a magician. He also got a black old-fashioned top hat. I made him a black cape lined in red.

Scott was reading magic books. We bought more magic tricks for him in Salzburg, Austria. One trick required a real rabbit. Well, my mom went with Scott to a pet store and came home with a rabbit. We got a cage for the rabbit and all the food and other supplies. The rabbit was gray and white and so cute. Scott spent a lot of time with the rabbit and did some tricks with him.

Scott also wanted some music as background to his tricks. He chose "Live and Let die" from the James Bond movie and used this piece for his Samba ball trick.

After he was well rehearsed, he had his first show. I invited all my friends and Scott's friends to see the show. All went well except that the rabbit came out of the hat a bit too early, but no nobody noticed.

Back in Canada, Scott started a business to show his magic tricks for birthday parties. I became Magic Mom because I had to drive him to every event. I bought him a Sesame Street magic trick, and all the children loved it. He had different tricks for different ages. We made a list of all of his tricks. I placed an ad in the local paper, and the business boomed!

Every Monday, we went to the bank to deposit his earnings into his own bank account. When he turned fourteen, he had saved enough money to pay for his own sailboat. We sold his little Optimist Pram and bought a new boat, a Laser.

What happiness for Scott! He worked very hard for the money.

Sojourn with Heidi

Getting married to Fred Kirkwood, 1964.

My son, Scott, 2 years old, 1968.

Heidi Leitner Fearon

My mom in Salzburg with Scott, 1970.

Magician Scott with his rabbit, 1974.

Sojourn with Heidi

My brother and me at my mother's 80th birthday, 1983.

Manfred, mom and me together, 1984.

10

Fred Leaving Time Magazine to Start CHIMO Magazine

Scott was growing up and becoming a fine young man. He was very involved with sailing, sports, music, and of course, his magic career. During this same time, Fred and I were reassessing our life together and his career. Fred was very concerned about his employment opportunities. Although Fred was a great salesman, it was becoming more and more difficult for him to capture his share of the advertising market. Things were changing. The market was different, the competition was younger, and the magazine management style was under review. *Time* magazine wanted to transfer Fred to another city in the United States because his job in Canada was being eliminated. They needed him in a new location. Fred did not want to leave Canada, so he decided to start his own magazine. While considering all the changes that were to come, I recorded my thoughts in a poem:

> *Is life so difficult like people say?*
> *How can I believe it, what a beautiful day.*
> *The sky is blue, the air soft and warm,*
> *nobody is here who could do me harm.*
>
> *The telephone, yes, I can hear it ring,*
> *and here's the milkman, do I need a thing?*
> *His bill is high, how can this be?*
> *Please stop the world, I want to be free.*

Yes, these are things one has to see.
Sometimes I think we work together to be free.
But freedom is something nobody can buy,
the battle goes on even with gin or rye.

Starting our own magazine would come to be a major chapter in our lives. *CHIMO* magazine was a giveaway publication for the elite. Its survival was based strictly on its advertisements. Fred was a great salesman and was solely responsible for obtaining the ads. He had done a very good job for *Time*, and now he had to do the same for himself. This was a monumental task, and he worked very hard to accomplish his goal. Finally, volume 1, number 1, was published in 1978.

"*CHIMO*"

To the Inuit of the Ungava Peninsula, the word (pronounced "Cheemo") is an Eskimo greeting meaning "are you friendly?"

Scott was twelve years old and very proud of his father and what his father was doing with the magazine. I continued to work, and Scott was attending Loyola High School. Loyola was a school for boys, and they all wore the uniform of the school. I drove Scott to school every day, but he walked home. There was never any question as to where Scott would be after school. If he wasn't at home, he was at the computer room at the university. Scott was mesmerized by computers and all that he could learn from them. He organized his magic tricks for the different ages on a computer. It was all so new.

My husband bought a computer for *CHIMO*. The computer was very large! What a difference from the technology of today. Fred put all of his *Time* magazine severance money into *CHIMO*. The first year, he had enough advertisements to make a profit. Going forward, we monitored our profit/loss experience on a month-by-month basis. Being an independent entity was a challenge with regard to meeting operating costs. The marketplace was changing, and the stresses of promoting a new magazine were extraordinary.

CEGEP was an educational requirement for students living in Quebec who wanted to attend university. Scott attended a boarding school, Champlain College, which was the mandatory requirement he needed to fulfill before entering university.

Heidi Leitner Fearon

With Scott away at school, I decided I could help Fred with the magazine for one year. I had to give notice to my boss and leave a profession that I truly loved and friends I had grown to know and enjoy.

The train station was close to the house, so I decided to take the train to work at the magazine. This allowed me to save money on parking since Fred had only one parking spot in the office garage. The office was in the Mount Royal Hotel across from Seagram's headquarters in downtown Montreal. It was a great space and location. I worked very hard hand-delivering the first issue of our magazine to our important clients. I did this every month.

We hired many freelance writers to create articles for the magazine. I worked closely with them and learned a lot from them.

It was a very busy time in my life. However, I had another big project to accomplish. My mom's eightieth birthday was approaching, and the city of Salzburg was honoring my mother. She was to become an honorable citizen of Austria for her accomplishments as a writer, a poet, and the president of the writers' society called "Die Silberrose" (meaning the Silver Rose). The date was March 2, 1983.

I wanted to plan a special event for my mom. My mother had three brothers and one sister in East Berlin. Another sister lived in Hamburg. The wall divided East Berlin from the West. I wanted to find a way for my mom's brothers and sisters to attend the big honoring ceremony. I had never had an opportunity to meet them. My grandfather had passed away a few years earlier. I had met him once when I was little, before the Berlin Wall was built.

My aunt Heidi and her husband helped me to get permission from Russia to allow the siblings to visit my mom for this occasion. Only the brothers, without their wives, and the one sister were allowed to come for six days. Aunt Traudi was not married. I had to pay for their transportation. They were not allowed to bring any East Berlin money with them. It took forever to get this organized, my goal being to surprise my mother.

My aunt Heidi, her husband Kurt, and their two sons would be traveling together. Uncle Gerhard would not have a problem traveling from Hamburg. There was a very quaint pension just across the street from the location of the ceremony. They made reservations in the pension on Rainberg.

Sojourn with Heidi

The East Berlin situation was a different problem. One of the brothers wanted to travel alone. This was fine, but they all had to arrive the same day. I gave them the "red carpet" treatment when they arrived, bringing a little red carpet with me for when I greeted them at the train station. I was at the train station most of the day, and my brother drove the guests to our house so they could get settled. A friend of mine entertained my mother for the day so she wouldn't know what was going on.

Two of the brothers, Gorhard and Ernst, had to stay together in one room. This was the only room with twin beds. I did not know that they'd had a fight about twenty years earlier and were not speaking to each other. They had to speak to each other now—they would be sleeping in the same room! It turned out they had forgotten what the fight was all about and became brothers again.

Traudi and brother Helmut stayed together in another room. We borrowed a mattress to put on the floor for Uncle Helmut. Then there was another problem: they were all vegetarians! I thought, *What a waste of all this great Austrian food.*

But they all liked pastries. Austria had plenty of pastries! Thanks to all my friends, we had homemade desserts every day. Everyone helped. My brother's wife Edith and I made different vegetable soups. Great teamwork! The big evening for my mother's award was scheduled for the day after they all arrived.

The event was held in the big marble hall where many civil marriages were performed. My brother had married in this beautiful hall. It was the most festive place, fit for a queen. My brother took my mom to the hairdresser, and I smuggled the gang out of the house. Our family's house was very large. It had a central stairway, but my mom lived in another wing of the house.

Now came the big night. I dressed Mom all in pale blue. I had designed the dress in Canada and bought the accessories in Salzburg. She wore pale blue nylon stockings and a matching scarf. She looked great!

Mom prepared her speech with my brother and me, and then we went together to the festive place. I was supposed to be with them but had to look after the rest of the gang. After we all had a bite to eat, I went early to the marble hall with all the relatives and lined them up in the first row.

The mayor of Salzburg introduced my mother, and she gave her speech.

Heidi Leitner Fearon

At that time I was trembling in my shoes. I had asked the mayor of Salzburg to introduce each one of my mother's brothers and sisters, explaining that this was a surprise for my mother. I had told him about all the work I'd done with government offices so they could be here temporarily from East Berlin for this occasion. I had given him a list with the names of all the brothers and sisters—Traudi, Helmut, and Ernst from East Berlin, then Gerhard and Heidi from Hamburg—as well as my brother Manfred's name.

The mayor introduced my brother and me. After my mother's speech, Mom received her honors. She received the old Salzburg city seal, a beautiful box with the city seal carved on it, and also the honorable Austrian citizen cross that she would wear for formal occasions. The crowd was clapping. They were so excited about my mother's achievements. This occasion had been written up in the local paper, and I think there were about 150 people present. Others in attendance were friends from the poets' society as well as other friends and neighbors. My son Scott was unable to attend because he was sixteen and attending college.

Then the moment came, and the mayor said, "There is just one more thing." He searched his jacket and brought out the list of all the names of her brothers and sisters. He looked at my mom and said, "For this occasion, Frau Leitner, there is another surprise for you!" He unfolded the paper and announced the name of the first brother, Ernst. Ernst stood up, and my mother started to cry. "Frau Leitner, there is more," the mayor said, and he very slowly introduced the rest of the siblings. I started to cry.

My mom went to each one of them, and the applause never stopped. She sank onto a stool and cried with all her siblings surrounding her. My brother and I were introduced last. I wore a red silk dress that I had made for the occasion.

At the end of the evening, we all walked home together and reminisced about our lives.

The remainder of our time together was one big party. My uncle Helmut spent every day in the large hardware store, buying all kinds of things he could not purchase in East Berlin. I told him to buy whatever he wanted but to remember he had to carry it all home. And carry it he did!

The relatives could not believe all the wonderful fruits and vegetables available to us at the local market; it was overwhelming for them. Our time together passed quickly. The brothers were reunited and friends again. We all got to know one another, but six days was not long enough.

After they all left, my mom kept asking me, "How did you do it?" It just proves you can do anything if it's really important—just work hard and plan well. I wanted this to be a perfect day for my mom, so it was! Friends helped by keeping my mom occupied when I needed to get things organized. This was definitely one of my greatest accomplishments (with a lot of help!).

11

An Old Friendship Evolves—Cal

After helping Fred out with the business for one year (without pay), I went back to work in my field. Fred was spending a lot of time in Toronto, and my job was often taking me to New York City.

Although Fred and I continued to enjoy going to the Thousand Islands, over time I felt we were drifting apart. He was borrowing money to continue with the magazine. He borrowed from his brothers and sisters. Fred was getting ads for the magazine, but payment came in the form of merchandise. For example, advertisements for Aquascutum Raincoats were paid for with raincoats but no actual cash. Our Air France advertisements allowed us to fly free first class but otherwise brought in no cash reimbursements. After ten years, the *CHIMO* magazine came to an end, and our marriage suffered under the strain.

There was one incident in Salzburg when Fred locked himself in my mother's bathroom with a bottle of Scotch. I was not at home, but my mother put Fred's suitcase in front of the door and told him to get out of her house. I was devastated. My mom said he had no manners, and I deserved better. I flew back to Canada. After this incident, alcohol became his dear friend, and I was considering a divorce.

We had been married for twenty-two years. Fred was a good man. He loved Scott, whom he called his prince, and Scott loved his father. We still visited the Thousand Islands and frequently spent time with our friends.

Although things were not going well with our marriage, I agreed to meet Fred at the island one weekend. When I arrived, I found him by the dock, drunk. Our neighbors, Cal and Cynthia, had been our friends for years. We had gotten to know each other very well and spent many weekends together on the island. Cal was aware of Fred's drinking problem. One day I went over to see Cal and asked if he would help me get Fred up the stairs and into bed. Cal was very sympathetic. I knew something similar was happening with his marriage. Cal's wife Cynthia had a significant problem with alcohol, and he was tired of her drunken episodes. So that day Cal said, "Let's go out on the boat and leave the two of them alone."

We went out for a boat ride and celebrated my birthday. This was the day Cal asked me if I would marry him.

My mom was hoping that I would move back to Austria after my divorce. But this was not going to happen. After Cal asked me to marry him, we spent more time getting to know each other. We had never had an affair prior to this time; we had never even kissed. But over the next year we got to know each other very well and trusted each other. I went back to Austria to see my mom. I had to tell her all about Cal.

I arrived in Salzburg and was sitting on my mom's balcony having coffee when the phone rang. The call was from a clerk at the Goldener Hirsch Hotel, who said a package had been delivered there for me. I didn't understand why a package would be sent to this very nice hotel, but I went down to pick it up. The hotel was only a few minutes away from my mother's home, so I walked there. I went to the front desk to ask for my package, and there it was! Cal was standing there with a big smile on his face. We hugged, and Cal said, "I want to meet your mother and ask her if she approves of me."

We walked hand in hand back to my mom's house, and when we greeted her together, I couldn't say a word through the tears running down my cheeks. Finally, I could talk. I said, "Mom, this is Cal."

My mom understood it was Cal from America. Yes, Cal from America! He had followed me here because he wanted to meet my mom. We sat down with Mom, and although she spoke very little English, I could tell she liked Cal. He asked her if it would be okay if he married me. Mom told him, "If Heidi approves, I would love to see you marry!"

I moved into the hotel with Cal, and that week we spent every day with Mom. I then stayed with my mom for another week. Cal sent my mother the biggest flower bouquet, with a card saying, "Thank you for Heidi. Cal."

Back in Canada we had to face a very difficult time in our lives. Both of us had to get divorced. It wasn't easy, but we did it, and finally, Cal and I were free to marry.

Cal was born in 1938 in Oneida, New York. He graduated from Syracuse University in 1960. He was affiliated with the Delta Kappa Epsilon fraternity and was active in the University Alumni Association. He was also a West Pointer. He served in the Air Force and later with the 174th Tactical Fighter Wing, the "Boys from Syracuse." He was now a lieutenant colonel in the reserves, so every weekend I saw him in his flight uniform.

Cal was the president of Syracuse Suburban Gas Company and a director of Oneida Valley National Bank. He had a very impressive career. Our life together was just beginning.

One day when we were together, Cal said, "I have some good news and some bad news."

I said, "Okay, I want the good news first."

"We will inherit Admiral," he said, referring to his black Labrador.

Now I wondered, what would be the bad news? Then he told me we were getting custody of Rena, his fourteen-year-old daughter. She did not want to live with her mother anymore.

I told him I didn't think that was bad news. I loved Rena and had always wanted a daughter. I told him that as long as he was a good dad and partner, all would be good.

July 17, 1987, was our big day—we got married! It was lovely. We married in the Thousand Island Park, with Cal's parents as our special guests. We all went out on the Bertram (our thirty-six-foot power boat) and celebrated with champagne and all the trimmings for the occasion. We told the children only after the fact. All went well with the children, although Cal's ex-wife was not happy because Rena was choosing to live with us.

All I wanted as I started out my marriage was the chest my father had made for me and my sewing machine. Scott brought me my Bernina sewing machine when I was still in my Montreal apartment. I still can't be without a sewing machine.

Cal wanted to build a house in Syracuse, but we had no idea where. He had a small airplane, so he flew to Montreal so we could meet and select the right place to build our new home. We always traveled with our dog Admiral.

Cal told me his new office was in East Syracuse. Not far from the office was a man-made lake. I thought it would be wonderful to build a house on the lake. There was a new development near the Erie Canal called Erie Village. A week later, Cal bought a lot on the water where we would build our house. I chose a house from a picture, and we also selected the tiles for the bathrooms, the wood flooring, and the bricks for the fireplace.

I was still working while they were finishing up the house. Before we got married, I had rented an apartment in Montreal. One day Cal came to the office and told me to pack up all my belongings, including the plant he had sent me. He said he'd tell me the details later.

Once we were out of the office, he told me, "You are done working." He did not like my new boss. I had given my employer three months' notice for a two-week vacation because we were chartering a sailboat, and the boss had refused the vacation request. On Monday morning Cal sent them a balloon-o-gram. He sang the song himself: "Take your job and shove it. She doesn't work here anymore." That was the end of my employment for that company. Everything from that point on would be new and different.

I had found the love of my life and was very happy. Scott was growing up and was at Queen's University in Kingston, Ontario. He worked at the university for one year and met a lovely girl from Brazil named Renata.

On weekends, we'd take the boat to Kingston to visit, and Scott and Rena would go out with us on the water. Rena was competent around boats and could manage her own small boat herself. We anchored in the bay and went swimming. Our dog Admiral was always with us.

We had a little dinghy so we could get Admiral ashore to do his business. One day in the morning, Admiral was barking, and we realized the dinghy had come untied and drifted away. We saw the boat in the distance, and Cal said he'd swim to get it. This was Admiral's transportation to get ashore, and we had to get it back. Cal had to rescue the dinghy. Cal was a very good swimmer, and he took a life preserver with him. He got the dinghy back, and we had a very happy dog!

12

A New Start

I was now Heidi the married lady. Scott was in college, and I had a fourteen-year-old daughter living with me. It was a totally new experience Thanks to Cal and our love for each other, our life was wonderful. We had the house in the Thousand Islands and our new home in Syracuse, New York.

Rena was a wonderful addition to my life. I loved having a daughter. Learning to cope with a teenager added a new dimension to my life. Cal was wonderful and very involved with his daughter. I loved to hear her practicing the saxophone. It brought back memories of all the musical events I had enjoyed in my home as a child.

The house was on the water, so we could go for a swim anytime, day or night. Of course, we always had Admiral with us. He was my new buddy and best friend. He loved to swim as well. We joined the local tennis club, signed up for a painting class, and met many new friends.

I now had a station wagon so Admiral could travel with me. He had a bed in the back, and I always had fresh water for him. I left the back window open just enough so that he could put his nose outside and smell the fresh air.

I had a radio connection with Cal's office because I had to find my way around Syracuse. That helped me a lot because I often had trouble finding addresses and getting lost. But it didn't take long before I felt comfortable driving through all the neighborhoods in town.

Having a second home was new to me. We had to drive about two hours to get to the Thousand Islands, and Lindock Island was in Canada.

Sojourn with Heidi

Most of the time, we kept the Bertram 36 in Canada, but often we would cross the border. Other times we left the boat in the Thousand Island Park, where Cal's parents had a summer cottage with a dock. All we had to do was call the border staff to let them know that we were on our way to our place on Lindock Island. What a great place that was.

At our home on the island, Cal had a separate house on the property for the children. In addition to his daughter Rena and his adopted son Jason, he had another daughter who lived in Australia. She was from Cal's first marriage. His first wife died of a brain tumor. We always had a lot of children around.

At our dock we had a slide and a diving board set up by the water. We had a big dock, so we were able to accommodate lots of boats. We enjoyed water skiing and other water sports.

We also had a hot tub, which was very popular, especially when the weather was cooler in the spring and fall. The main house was beautiful. It was an A-frame with a view to die for. We had huge ten-foot flowerpots in which we planted about eighty red geraniums. I was so proud of my plants, and I loved caring for them. We had many people visit from Montreal, including Erika, Carol, Dorte, and her family. There were so many others.

One late evening, we found the music at the children's house to be very loud—it was one o'clock in the morning! Cal and I decided to walk over to the house to turn the music down so we could go to bed. Well, there was nobody there! All the lights were on in the house, and the boats were docked, but no children were in sight. We decided to wait for them.

As parents we determined that the lights and loud music were for our benefit. The kids had been trying to give the impression that they were all at the house. Someone must have picked them up from the other side of the island. About 3:00 a.m., the gang walked in. We were sitting on the sofa without the lights on. At first they didn't see us. Then they turned the music off, and Cal stood up and walked over to them, initially saying nothing.

Jason greeted his dad with a big hello. But Dad only wanted to know where they'd been all night. They told us they had been at a friend's house for a party. Then came the inquisition—where were they, who picked them up, and so on. This would be the last time they'd leave the island at night with the music blasting and no one knowing their whereabouts. Everyone was sorry. Cal said he'd see them in the morning and added, "We will be staining the dock and steps—be ready."

Everyone got quiet, and we left. About 11:00 a.m. we woke everyone up, and we worked all day staining the dock and steps. After that they always asked if they could go to parties. We would take them and return for them later in the evening.

For a few years, we had a little Sunfish for sailing around the islands. But there was a change in the air. I had an inkling when Cal asked me the big question! "Heidi, what about selling the island house and the plane and buying a serious sailboat so we can sail anywhere in the world?"

I was completely surprised! "Cal," I said, "you only know how to sail the little Sunfish."

"Well, I know how to navigate, and you can teach me how to sail."

I was on the crew for schooner races in Nova Scotia, and I did know how to sail my other boat, the *Heidi-Ho*, a twenty-five-foot sailboat. But the idea of sailing alone in a much bigger boat with Cal gave me pause.

"Don't worry about a thing. I will learn fast," he told me. "This is something I've always wanted to do."

Rena was excited for us, as was Scott. Everyone thought it was a fine idea, but I knew this would involve much research and planning.

Getting married to Cal, 1987.

Sojourn with Heidi

My stepdaughter, Rena and Buffy, 1988.

13

Now the Big Boat

After much discussion and planning, we sold the island house and the plane, then traveled every weekend to find just the right boat for us. We finally found a Lafitte 44, a Bob Perry design, built in Taiwan. We found her in Marblehead, Massachusetts, and she was beautiful! She would be kept in Sackets Harbor on Lake Ontario, on the United States side. Our plan was to learn how to sail her on Lake Ontario and then the other Great Lakes.

First we had to transport the boat from Marblehead to Lake Ontario. This was a challenge. We motored most of the way. We had to get through many locks as we traveled up the St. Lawrence River. We both felt a great sense of accomplishment when we finally got into Sackets Harbor.

We had a big celebration when we arrived. Admiral, our dog, had been left at his favorite kennel while we were away. He hadn't seen the sailboat as yet, and I had concerns regarding his ability to adjust to sailing. But he had grown up on power boats and loved the water. He loved the Bertram and the Boston whaler.

The weekend following our arrival at Sackets Harbor, Admiral was introduced to the new boat. Well, a sailboat was a different story. The minute we turned on the engine, he started to shake. He was so scared. In addition, when the sails went up and the boat heeled, he panicked. He jumped on my lap like a small lapdog. Small, he was not!

What were we to do about Admiral? He traveled everywhere with us. Cal was convinced that he'd make the adjustment. This went on for a few summers as we sailed all of the Great Lakes.

Cal was a natural sailor and, of course, the best navigator. We loved our boat!

Since Cal was working full-time, we only had weekends to enjoy the boat.

Then one day we heard that Hurricane Hugo was coming our way and would threaten Sackets Harbor. We immediately drove to the harbor to prepare for heavy winds. We added three more big fenders to protect the boat from the dock. We put extra lines at the bow and the stern. We tied extra bungee lines around the sail covers, and so on and so on. There were many other boats in the harbor but not many people there. Some boats had very small lines securing the boats to the dock.

Cal carried every rope he could find on our boat into the cockpit in case we had to assist other boaters.

On September 23, 1989, the harbor was hit with the heavy winds from Hugo.

Early in the day it was calm, and we thought nothing was going to happen. Then all of a sudden, late in the afternoon, the wind started to howl. We had up to 80 mph winds. I hooked myself onto the railing so I would not blow off the boat.

Within fifteen minutes all six of our fenders popped. Cal turned on the engine so he could direct the boat away from the dock.

Cal had been wise to gather extra lines because we now had to help secure some of the untethered boats. It was a mess. Cal had enough spare lines to secure some of the other boats, but we finally ran out of lines. We did all that we could and worked for about five hours until the wind finally calmed. Exhausted, we went to bed on the boat.

The next morning, we awoke and were able to assess the damage. Again, what a mess! We had saved four other boats, and the owners were so grateful. Some boats were badly damaged, and a few were underwater. When some of the owners showed up that morning, they couldn't believe all that had happened.

The first thing we did was buy six new fenders. This was the only damage we had incurred. This taught us a lesson—you can't fight the weather; you can only prepare for it.

Cal's fraternity was Delta Kappa Epsilon, and the design of the spinnaker was his fraternity crest. It was blue on the outside with a red border and yellow in the middle. A big black lion was embedded on the yellow background. When the spinnaker arrived and we looked at it, it was a gorgeous sight! When we raised the spinnaker for the first time, I was able to take pictures from another boat of our boat and spinnaker, and it was beautiful. I think we paid $7,000 for that project, but boy, was it worth it.

Onshore, another domestic challenge was presented to me. Rena needed a prom dress. She showed me a picture of a Christian Dior dress she really loved. Its price was about $7,000 too! I said, "I like the dress. I can make it for you."

"No way," Rena said.

I told her I could make the dress, but I would need her help. She had no idea how she could help! First, we had to find the fabric, and then she would have to help me make the pattern.

She chose a black halter dress with a flower on the right shoulder. It had a full crepe double skirt. We needed ten yards of fabric. All the edges had to be embroidered. We bought a corselet that fit and looked great on Rena. The corselet was the foundation, and now it needed to be covered by fabric. I added a zipper on the side to allow for ease in dressing.

The flower at the top corner of the dress would be embroidered. The body of the gown was logicated and stitched to a very dramatic skirt. The edges of the skirt were all hand-embroidered, a very time-consuming project. After three weeks of work, the dress was finished! When Rena came home from school, I had the dress on my dress form (a dummy). She couldn't believe it. She yelled, "You did it!"

We bought very pretty black shoes to complete the outfit. Rena got dressed with her new dress for the first time. She had beautiful long red hair, and she looked elegant! Did I mention the flower on the dress, all embroidered at the edges, with the help of my Bernina sewing machine? I have a lovely picture of Rena going off to her prom. Cal couldn't believe that I had made the dress, one of a kind, an original!

As for me, I was still playing lots of tennis. One day, friends and I were set to play doubles, and one of the girls did not show. I went to the reception desk to advise that we needed another player. The woman said she might have a fourth player for us. I went back to the court. The new addition arrived and introduced herself as Billie. One of my friends asked if she was Billie Jean King. Yes, she was! Oh my God, did we have a treat.

She rotated play with everyone and gave us some great tennis tips. She happened to be in Syracuse for an exhibition match. She was so nice to help us out. What a great day that was. What a great lady!

Now in my free time, and there wasn't much of that, I was taking watercolor painting lessons. I did this once a week. At the end of the year, we had an exhibition. During that time we could sell our paintings. Cal asked me not to sell them because he loved my paintings. All the art pieces were nicely framed, and visitors could meet the artists. I put a high price on my paintings, thinking they would never sell. The next day, after the show, the instructor called me to say that two of my paintings had sold. Oh boy, how would I tell Cal?

Cal came home for lunch that day, and we talked and talked, and finally, just as he was leaving to go back to work, I said, "I am sorry, but two of my paintings sold."

He said, "Oh really, do you know the buyer?"

Of course, I did not know the name of the buyer. Cal placed his hand in mine and led me to the door of our stairwell. There were my two paintings. He told me that someone had offered the asking price, so he had bought them back at a higher price. He didn't want me to sell them. Well, as of today I still have those two paintings.

I thought I'd add the following story as a warning to you regarding swimming in unfamiliar ponds and other waters. Know the water conditions before you decide to take a swim. One day I realized I had developed a terrible itch behind my knees, in the crook of my arms, and in other warm parts of my body. We had a very nice friend who happened to be a physician. I told him about my problem. He thought I was having an allergic reaction to the diesel fumes from the boat or chemicals used on the boat. It was not unusual for me to take a swim after working on the sailboat. I liked to swim in our lake.

I was examined by several physicians over a three-month period, but the problem persisted. The final physician asked me where I went swimming. I told him I swam in the pond in front of our house. He felt a biopsy was necessary to better understand what was causing my itchy welts. A few days later, he told me what was wrong. I had parasites under my skin, infecting the areas. He told me that a large number of Canada geese common to the area frequently landed on the ponds and beaches and

Heidi Leitner Fearon

left their droppings in the water. The water was often contaminated with different parasites. My welts were filled with parasites!

The doctor called the condition "duck itch." Once we knew the source of the problem, I was cured quickly. Who ever would have known about duck itch? I never swam in that pond again.

14

Selling the Suburban Gas Company

My husband's grandfather, Harry Carver, had bought the Suburban Gas Company in 1925. The company was based in East Syracuse and had 4,500 customers.

Its major customers were Bristol Myers Squibb Co., Carrier Corp, and Chrysler Corp. My husband Cal was the current president and chief executive officer of Suburban Gas. The company now had eleven million dollars in revenues.

Niagara Mohawk (NiMo) was interested in purchasing Suburban Gas. NiMo had 475,000 gas customers and wanted to further expand the company.

After many days of negotiations, the deal was agreed upon, and all principals authorized the sale. The actual date of the sale was April 30, 1992.

After the sale, Cal was offered a position with NiMo, but Cal had made the decision to sell the company for a very special reason. We had learned to sail the new boat, passed our scuba diving tests, and secured our offshore sailing licenses—we were ready to set sail and work no more! We decided not to sell the house in Syracuse until we were certain that sailing offshore would be as much fun as we expected.

Our first ocean trip would be with the Caribbean 1500 from Newport to Bermuda.

Steve Black organized that offshore sail. Our daughter Rena was starting college at the Hartt School of music, so her life was settled. There was only one big problem: we could not take Admiral, our black Labrador retriever, with us. He was just a lover and the greatest dog, but he did not like the sailboat. He still holds a special place in my heart, so I have decided to include a few stories about Admiral.

Admiral was a good-size Labrador retriever; however, in times of trouble, he became a lap dog, and my lap was where he sought comfort! He loved the house on the water because he loved to swim. Sometimes he got out of the house on his own and would run around the lake and into the woods.

One day I noticed he was missing. I looked everywhere but could not find him. Then came a phone call from our kennel. The woman from the kennel said, "Admiral just checked in. Do you want him to have a bath? He's very dirty." He was a regular customer, and they loved him. Of course, I said yes. They would call me when his treatment was done. Later that day, I went to the shop to find a very clean, very happy dog.

I was puzzled as to how he had gotten to the kennel. After a few days, we went out for a walk, this time with Admiral on his leash. I walked him through the woods, hoping to discover the route he had taken to the kennel. Yes, Admiral knew his way. Unfortunately, his route involved a very muddy path. But there, next to the creek, was the kennel.

He always wore a dog collar tagged with his name, address, and phone number. Given that he was an escape artist, this was a very wise investment.

At Christmastime we had placed an Advent wreath on the dining room table. It was the fourth day of Advent, so I had four candles lit—real candles! Cal and I were going to a Christmas party in Oneida, New York, and Admiral would be left at home to guard the house. Before leaving the house, Cal wet his fingers and extinguished the candles. Admiral had his bed, water, and toys in the entrance hallway. We gave him his treat, and off we went. We never locked the door with Admiral there. He was trained by Cal to guard the house and let no one in.

We had a wonderful time at the party. It was snowing when we left for home.

When we arrived at the house, we saw a fire truck out in front of our house and Admiral being walked by one of the firemen. Oh my God! My first thought concerned the candles. Well, one of the candles had not been fully extinguished, and the Advent wreath had caught on fire, fallen onto the table, burned the tablecloth, and fallen onto the chairs, causing a house fire.

Since the door was not locked, the firemen hadn't had to break the door to get in. The smoke alarm must have gone off, signaling the fire department to come to the house. Rena was with us, so the only one in harm's way was Admiral. There was so much smoke that all the windows had to be opened. All I could do was cry while holding on to Admiral, so grateful that he was safe. After the firemen and everyone else left, we made arrangements to have everything cleaned. Rena made us both a stiff drink!

What a day that was! We hired a service company to clean up the house, wash the walls, and so on. They were incredible and managed to get rid of the smoke smell completely. They had a crew of four people, and after two days of hard work, they had everything back to normal.

The firemen had used some type of spray to extinguish the fire, so there was no water damage. We did need to purchase a new carpet. I started sewing new curtains for the dining room and kitchen. Everything worked out fine. We were so happy Admiral had survived the event.

Admiral was trained to obey word commands. One of those commands was "forget it." When we had food on the table, all we had to say was "forget it!" He would then sit down or walk away. He would never touch any food if we told him to forget it. One day I baked six layers of cake for a very special Austrian cake called a Dobosch cake. I put the six layers onto wax paper so they could cool. Then I went off to play tennis. But I forgot to tell Admiral to forget it before I left. When I came home to finish the cake for my dinner party, three layers were missing. I could not find Admiral anywhere. He always greeted me when I came home. I went upstairs into the bedroom, and there he was, a very guilty dog, hiding behind the bed.

Well, it was my fault. I should have said "forget it," and I'm sure he would not have touched the cake. On a brighter note, I finished the cake with the remaining three layers, and it still tasted very good. This was just one of many funny, memorable stories about Admiral.

When Admiral was ten years old, we were planning our long sailing trip, so special plans had to be considered for Admiral. We knew we could not take him sailing, yet we wanted him to be safe, loved, and happy. After weighing many options, we called his breeder. She was a very nice lady and said she had kept one of his sisters for herself and would keep Admiral for us. Of course, our Admiral came with a trust fund.

One week before our departure, we met the breeder in a parking lot. We brought all of Admiral's belongings—his bed, toys, food, treats, and so on. She had a van that opened in the back, and everything including Admiral went in the back of the van. The door was still open, and Admiral was ready to jump out to go with us. I gave him one last big hug, and Cal said, "Forget it!" The dog did not move as we drove off. I had never cried so much!

We knew he would be well cared for, but we missed him so much. I called the kennel several times before we left and was told by the breeder that Admiral loved his sister and was settling nicely into his new life. It was still a heartbreak for me. I still think about him.

We worked very hard to put everything onto our boat for our big departure.

The house had to be cleaned and everything readied for this major transition. My back was hurting from all the lifting and other physical work. The doctor told me I had a slipped disc and to be careful lifting. There was so much more to do. I couldn't worry about a slipped disc.

My last task before leaving was to write letters of goodbye to all my friends and family. I was on the boat, handing a friend of mine some letters to put into the mailbox. Rena was untying the line, and people were screaming goodbyes as we prepared to leave the dock. All of a sudden, Cal yelled to me to duck my head as the boom pushed across the deck. Well, the boom didn't hit my head as it crossed the deck—it hit my back! I held onto the railing to keep from falling overboard.

I had a big bruise on my back, but the amazing part of the story is that ever since that accident, I've never had any more problems with my back! Of course, I would not recommend this kind of fix for a slipped disc. I was lucky that it worked for me!

Now we were on our way to Newport, Rhode Island. It was September 25, 1992. This would be our first offshore sailing experience, from Newport to Bermuda. Before we left the dock, I called my mom in Austria. She wished us all the best.

Now we were on our way, my backache was resolved, and we could begin to relax and enjoy our newfound freedom.

Sojourn with Heidi

We sailed down Lake Ontario and went through several locks passing through Montreal. As we sailed down the Saint Lawrence, the river widened, and the shoreline seemed further and further away. I was at the helm when all of a sudden I saw a big whale jump out of the water and flip onto his back. What a beautiful sight! We saw so many whales along the way.

Further down the river, we sailed to Prince Edward Island. I knew the place very well because Fred, Scott, and I had spent several summers vacationing there. I loved that island. We motored very slowly as we searched for the dock. Fishermen were out everywhere. We also encountered many lobster traps, requiring us to keep a close watch. It was like a minefield. However, the good news is that we made it through without getting tangled on anything.

After Prince Edward Island, we were off to Brador Lake. We found a beautiful cove in which to anchor. This location was a haven for bald eagles. They were as beautiful as the surrounding scenery. We used the dinghy to explore the area. In town was the great Graham Bell museum, which we visited.

I learned quickly how to prepare meals on a boat, and it was lots of fun.

Our next stop was Halifax, another area I knew well. I had learned how to crew on sailing schooners out of the Second Peninsula in Nova Scotia. David Stevens built all his own schooners. I had been lucky enough to meet him and his family and to sail with them.

We had to limit our sightseeing at this point because we had to get to Newport, Rhode Island, at a designated time. Up to this point, we'd had fair weather, but it got cold at night. We still had a long way to go.

15

The Caribbean 1500

We arrived at Newport on October 15. We found the marina and met up with the other twelve yachters who would be involved in the Caribbean 1500 rally to Bermuda.

The distance to Bermuda was about 1,500 nautical miles, a five-day offshore sail. The twelve yachts were all different types and sizes. It was very important that the rigging be strong enough for offshore sailing. Every boat was inspected by a professional, and quite a few boat owners had to spend significant amounts of money to ensure proper rigging. We all had to attend a course every day to learn about everything that could go wrong. Steve Black was the instructor. He had the experience of sailing all around the world. We had to have our life rafts inspected and had to learn how to store the dinghy correctly. Flares had to be in working order just in case we needed them. Our radio had to work properly because we would need to communicate with each other twice a day. We would maintain radio contact and report our positions to one another.

There was a nice gentleman from Canada named Herb. He would contact us by radio twice a day to give a full report on the weather conditions.

Next, we had to review the provisions necessary for the trip. I remember that we bought so much food that it lasted for a long time. I precooked many of our meals so that all we would have to do was reheat them. I had some experience doing this type of food preparation. The important thing was not to get seasick.

We got to know the people traveling with us very well since we were all taking the same courses together.

Following are the names of all the yachts that participated:

> *Navire* (the largest one)
> *Troubadour*
> *Nomad*
> *Cathexis LL*
> *Tai-Pan* (we are still great friends with the owners, whose dinghy was named *Tied On*)
> *Zephyr 1*
> *Charade*
> *Midnight Wave*
> *Aries Won* (this was our boat—Cal was an Aries, and he always won)
> *Between the Sheets* (we're still friends with this couple; we always said they spent a lot of time between the sheets!)
> *MB Three*
> *Harmony* (still friends, still sailing together)

There was a gentleman from Syracuse named Tom on one of the boats. He knew Cal from Syracuse. He owned a chain of very prosperous car washes. After one of our briefings, Tom asked to talk to us. We went for lunch and listened to his proposition. He asked Cal if there was any way he could sail with us to Bermuda. He told us his wife Susan would be joining him in Bermuda, and they would like to sail with us to St. Thomas.

The boat he was supposed to sail with was the *Navire*, and he said it was a mess. He told us the owner was a Navy Seal, but he was crazy. My eyes lit up because Tom had done offshore sailing, and so had his wife Susan.

I trusted Cal completely, but one extra experienced sailor on board was the answer to my prayers. I was so scared of having so much to do with only Cal and me on board. Our answer was yes, and Tom settled into his quarter—what a relief!

We had our charts in order in the navigation station, our radar was working fine, and we were ready to go.

We had one more dinner at the Chart House with Bob, his wife Lee, and her mother Barbara. Their boat was the *Tai-Pan*. We became best friends. They also had a black Labrador retriever, but theirs loved to sail. The dog would be flown into St. Thomas to be with them on the boat. I cried again that night. I missed our Admiral so much.

On the evening of October 26, it was snowing! The plan was to set sail the very next day, and we did! There was a helicopter taking pictures of the yachts sailing off with all sails up. This was a big adventure for everyone.

On October 27, 1992, it was cold, but the sun was shining, and all was well. I will never forget that incredible day. We were officially off to the races, on our first offshore sailing trip!

We had our life preservers on. They were like horseshoe collars. If we had to use them, there was a cord to pull The life preserver would automatically inflate, and a light would flash. A whistle was attached in case one had to use it. We had learned all about boat safety at our daily lectures. When in the cockpit doing night watch, we'd attach ourselves with long and short secure tethers so we couldn't fall overboard. We had all sails up and were ready to reef if we had to. We also had a storm jib ready just in case.

In the cockpit, I had a cooler bag with many different snacks for whoever was on night shift. This included small cans of Vienna sausages, granola snacks, coffee, water to drink, chocolate bars, and so on. I was below, getting ready for our first meal, when all of a sudden I heard thunder and saw lightning. The waves were getting bigger and bigger, and I was scared!

I asked Tom, "What is going on? Are we going to be all right?"

He told me not to worry; the storm would pass. He told me we were crossing the Gulf Stream, and this location made its own uncertain weather. I worried that the lightning would hit our mast. Tom told me to stay below—he and Cal had everything under control. Oh boy, I was trembling in my boat shoes and was hoping this wouldn't last long. They reefed the main sail, but the boat was still rocking like hell! I thought this lasted forever, but forever was only about four hours.

I heard Cal yell, "Did you see that wave?" It was a big one; I felt it below.

Suddenly, the storm was over, the ocean was calm, and I went up to put

Sojourn with Heidi

my head into the cockpit. Tom and Cal were laughing and said, "Let's have a beer!" The good news was nothing happened, and no one got seasick. It was a good test. It was time for me to make us something to eat.

With all the sails up, we continued our voyage to Bermuda. The wind was blowing steadily. We talked twice a day with all the other boats and got their positions. After a few hours at sea, we never saw another boat traveling with the Caribbean 1500. We did see some freighters and a cruise ship, but other than that, not much else. We all did our watches, four hours on, four hours off. I was so grateful that we had Tom with us. He had done many offshore trips and calmed me down. I loved preparing the meals. It was fun and a challenge. The weather got warmer, and the attire became shorts and T-shirts!

We had a lot of bread on the boat, including croissants and coffee cakes. The third day out, I wanted to surprise the boys with freshly made bread. I had bought a box of bread dough for the bread-making machine. All I had to do was add warm water, knead the dough, and hope it would rise.

I put the bowl into my hanging basket, where the sun was shining, and surprise—the dough started rising. I punched it down one more time and then shaped it into a loaf. I also added some garlic and onions, then baked it in the oven.

When I removed the perfect bread from the oven, I put it on a wooden board with a knife on the side, a big chunk of Brie, and some homemade jam. Not only did the boat smell good, but you should have seen the boys when I brought the tray into the cockpit. Boy, was it good! That evening, when Cal spoke on the radio, he exclaimed, "Guess what Heidi made today?" Well, everyone now wanted to make bread. To this day, some of our sailing friends still talk about the perfect bread.

Our Canada connection, Herb, continued giving us the weather report, twice a day.

The weather was perfect all the way to Bermuda. We did not have to tack at all for the final two days. The most exciting moment was when I was sunning myself at the bow and could see land for the first time. I screamed, "Land ahoy!" The boys searched the sea with binoculars, and yes, we were approaching Bermuda. We let the sails out just a bit for the perfect approach. I went below to clean up and get ready for our landing at the Bermuda Yacht Club.

We were the second boat to arrive in Bermuda. I wanted to kiss the ground. When we stepped off the boat to walk on the dock, it felt like the dock was moving. After almost five days offshore, the feeling was weird. Tom's wife, Susan, had arrived from Syracuse and moved into her accommodations with her husband. We celebrated our first offshore crossing with a Dark and Stormy cocktail! This was a Bermuda rum drink made with Pusser's rum and Gosling ginger beer. What a new taste sensation! The next day, other boats arrived. Some needed repairs, and we all needed fuel and water.

We rented scooters to explore Bermuda. In Bermuda, we drove on the left side of the road, which was the opposite of what we did in the USA and Canada. As we were scooting along, someone came around the corner ahead of us on the wrong side of the road. We had to head for a bush on the side of the road. Thanks to Cal's fast reaction, we only ended up with a few scratches. I had a bump on my head, but that was all.

After a few days in Bermuda, and having watched all the boats arrive safely, we started to prepare for our next crossing: Bermuda to St. Thomas. This trip would be 956 nautical miles. Depending on the weather and wind, it would take four to five days. The weather was expected to be perfect according to Herb's predictions and daily weather reports.

Sojourn with Heidi

Our first Carribean 1500 trip to Bermuda with Aries Won, 1992.

16

We Are Off Again

Susan was handling the sails, Cal was at the helm, and Tom was at the navigation station, plotting our course to St. Thomas. We looked like a bunch of professional sailors. I had learned a lot from our sail from Newport. We set the sails for a perfect course, and now we could relax and let the wind do the job.

Susan, Tom, and Cal were laughing and were sure we'd sail into St. Thomas's Crown Bay Marina as number one. It was a rally after all, and why not come in first? I would be happy just to get there, but with this competitive crew, being first was part of the fun. Everything was checked all the time, we had all the sails up, including the spinnaker when needed, and boy, did we have some great speed. We now had four people for our day and night shifts—what a difference that made.

I was very happy to do the cooking. One day I was preparing a salad and found a bad tomato. I had a habit of throwing things overboard. There was an open hatch right over my head in the galley, so I decided to throw the tomato through the hatch. As I did, Cal was passing by, and the tomato hit him right in the face. "What are you doing?" Cal yelled.

I told him I was so sorry. I was just trying to dispose of a rotten tomato! We all had a good laugh from that incident. I never threw anything out the hatch again!

We could see land again. This time Susan yelled, "Land ahoy!" We all went to the cockpit to check it out. There were so many islands as we approached the area. I cleaned up the boat, and with great anticipation, we entered Crown Bay Marina as the number one boat!

Cal handed me the horn. I blew the horn as all the other boats sailed into the marina. Within the next two days, everyone arrived safely.

Crown Bay Marina was a large marina that could accommodate many mega-sized yachts. I have never seen that many beautiful yachts at one marina in my life.

Bob and Lee's dog arrived in St. Thomas, giving rise to thoughts of my dog Admiral. I called to see how he was and learned that all was well.

I called my mom in Austria and Scott in Canada to give them an update on our location. They were so happy to hear from us. Cal also called his family to be sure they were all well.

There was a bar in the marina called Tickles. I had my first Bushwacker at that bar. It was a very potent drink with lots of different types of alcohol. It tasted like a milkshake, but boy, you'd never want to have two of them! There was a cute sign at Tickles that read "Men don't get old, they just get a little dinghy."

We all had our dinghies launched, and like little kids, we explored the neighborhood. Across from the Crown Bay Marina, there was another island with a beautiful cove and beach called Honeymoon Cove. The ocean was so warm and refreshing that I wanted to stay there forever. We stayed for about five days in St. Thomas and then planned our next trip.

After shopping for fresh food and doing our laundry, we were ready to visit the British Virgin Islands. We learned all about checking in and out of customs. With our boat papers and passports safely inside a waterproof folder, off we went to explore the British Virgin Islands. Our focus was on finding the entrance so that we could secure the boat and then take the dinghy in to clear customs.

All was going well, and our first stop would be Tortola. We liked everything about the British Virgin Islands. Sir Francis Drake Channel was our main waterway to get from place to place. We also found a location that had tennis courts, and we stopped and played—that was fun!

We fell in love with Jost Van Dyke island and got to know Foxy's. This was our first experience with this bar. The bar had lots of rum, some juices, no ice, one light bulb, and three hammocks. But what fun we all had! When I visited Foxy's many years later, things had changed. The owner had become one very wealthy man. Foxy's was no longer just a bar. There was a gift shop and a dock for your boat or dinghy. It just wasn't the same.

Norman Island, Cooper Island, Virgin Gorda, and Anegada became our playing field. Each of these places was unique, which made them so special. Anegada had the greatest beach and the best lobsters. When going into the island, you had to pick up a buoy and secure your boat. We had fun watching other sailors sail in and attempt the task!

Christmas Cove was a favorite spot for us and many of our Caribbean 1500 friends. The snorkeling was fantastic, and the anchor held very well. A secure anchor was essential, and Cal always dove down to check on the position and security of the anchor.

Afternoon cocktails were a real treat. We all tied our dinghies together and passed around cocktails and appetizers. Everyone contributed something. When out on the open sea, we'd tie up together and drift along while watching the sunset. What a good time we had. We'd exchange stories and share our food and beverages. If someone wanted to return to their boat, they'd just untie and go home.

All the islands had a special charm. The more we liked the island, the longer we stayed. There was no set agenda—we were totally free.

I started quilting. I also painted little watercolor pictures of whatever caught my eye on the islands. I have so many wonderful watercolor paintings from this trip. And of course, I had my sewing machine with me, so I could work on any number of sewing projects.

Part of the fun of offshore sailing was the camaraderie you shared with the other sailors. Cal helped many boaters with repairs. A boat floating in salt water has many things that can break down. If anyone needed help fixing something on their boat, they could almost always find someone willing to help. We helped many sailors in need along the way.

Sojourn with Heidi

Christmas on Sojourner, 1996.

We lost Aries Won and bought a new boat, a Tyana 52 named Sojourner Passing the Twin Towers in New York, 1994.

17

Sailing the Caribbean Islands

We loved the British Virgin Islands, but we wanted to explore more of the US Virgin Islands.

When we returned to the US territory, we immediately went to the customs office to get clearance. We sailed to St. John, where I spotted a drum for the first time in my life. It's a very beautiful small fish. We'd often go off in our dinghy and explore different areas, snorkeling through a sea of beautiful fish and ocean flora.

We walked up to Ram's Head, and the view was beyond belief. Each sunset and ocean view was more beautiful than I ever could have imagined.

On our way back to the boat, we discovered a small trailer selling ice cream. What a treat that was. It happened to be Ben and Jerry's. We could see the island of St. Croix in the far distance. We were among about five boats in Leinster Bay. By now dinghy drifts had become a regular occurrence as we watched the most spectacular sunsets. We enjoyed each other's company so much that we decided to sail to Culebrita to celebrate Thanksgiving together.

We looked at the chart before entering the bay. There were lots of big rocks and coral reefs to watch for, but the reward of getting there was extra special. We all anchored behind a spectacular coral reef and stayed for a lovely two-week visit.

There weren't many people in this area. However, people from Puerto Rico with power boats knew about this jewel and powered into Culebrita at the end of the week. As many as twenty other boats joined us. They dropped two anchors, one on the beach and the other in the water.

Now their fun began. They brought windsurfers, rowing boats, small skidoos, and all sorts of dinghies. There were people water skiing and daring kids diving off their boats. Of course, snorkeling through the magnificent coral reef was both beautiful and exciting. We swam from our boat, well equipped with our flippers, and joined the very friendly group.

On Sunday afternoon, everybody left, and again we had Culebrita all to ourselves.

This beautiful beach was about a mile long, with the most precious turquoise water. We walked the beach every day. It was a pleasure to see that even though there were many visitors to the beach, it remained pristine, with no sign of litter anywhere. Everyone respected this little treasure.

Walking to the top of the island was very special. There was an old abandoned lighthouse there with a helicopter pad. Back at the beach, we discovered a round basin where big waves were splashing. We called it our jacuzzi. Bob and Lee and their dog Chelsea loved that place. Two weeks go by very fast when you are having fun!

There was one particularly beautiful experience I had when snorkeling. I was swimming alone, and all of a sudden, something swam right up to my mask. I was so startled. It was a dolphin. I snorkeled at least another thirty minutes, and the dolphin stayed with me. When I swam back to the boat, we separated. I was showering in the cockpit when I heard Cal shout, "There's the dolphin!" I came up to see, and there was the dolphin, swimming close to the boat. The dolphin stayed close to the boat and then performed one big jump before swimming off. I never saw him or her again.

Now we were off, with two other boats, to visit Puerto Rico's main island. Cal, being a military man, decided we'd sail to the military base, Roosevelt Roads. We sailed past Isla de Culebra and Isla de Vieques. Anchoring was easy for us. I had learned that art very quickly. Cal always dove down to check the anchor, and I got the nickname "the happy hooker"! We very seldom had an anchor problem.

We loved exploring Puerto Rico. Four of us rented a car, and off we drove.

After driving around the island, we walked all through the downtown area. It was exciting. We found a great restaurant for lunch and another quaint place, off of a side road, where we ate the best fajitas! Back on our boat, we celebrated this great day with my new cocktail, a Bushwacker.

We re-provisioned in the commissary the next day. The saleswoman asked me if we'd seen the manta rays, and we had not. She gave us directions to the location, and we were able to walk there. What we found was a large floating circle filled with lettuce. All the out-of-date salad from the markets got delivered to the manta rays. There must have been at least ten manta rays feeding. A small boat was there, from which men were tossing the lettuce into the floating ring. One of the men asked me if I'd like to swim with them. You know what my answer was! Into the water I went to swim with those beautiful creatures. I swam with them, petted them, and personally delivered them food—they let me do it! I had never experienced anything like it. It was a great opportunity, and I loved it!

Our next adventure would be St. Croix. However, first we were going to make a stop to scuba dive for lobsters. This was a first for us. Our friends Dick and Lisa knew where to find the lobsters and how to capture them. At first all I did was swim with them and watch them. I thought, *What is Dick doing swimming with a mop?* Well, he went down under the rocky shelf, and with his mop he caught a lobster. Needless to say, now I knew how to catch lobsters! The lobsters got tangled up in the mop, and you then brought them into the boat and checked them out. If there were any females, they had to be put back in the ocean. We caught lots of lobsters that day. We put them on the grill with garlic butter and served them with scrumptious bread and corn from the commissary. We stayed an extra day to find and freeze more lobsters.

There was a castle at the very top of the island that was absolutely beautiful. We anchored in the harbor, got into our dinghy, and went ashore to visit the yacht club bar. After asking a lot of questions, we learned that the beautiful castle belonged to Contessa Nadia Farber. I was painting my small watercolor paintings along the way, and I had to paint this view.

St. Croix had an underwater safari. As you snorkeled through the area, there were underwater plaques explaining what you were seeing—exotic fish, different coral formations, et cetera. You could snorkel all around the island, and the water was so warm and so clear. This became my new exercise regimen. Sometimes I couldn't stop. Swimming with those huge turtles was so fascinating. This is still one of my favorite places to snorkel.

Another lesson learned when swimming: do not wear any jewelry or anything shiny. The barracudas are attracted to shiny objects. You leave barracudas alone.

We also saw spotted eagle rays jumping in the evening, a view that blended with a perfect sunset. Add a glass of wine to the mix, and life couldn't get much better! Cheers! Of course, I was with my perfect husband and my great friends.

Now it was time to review our charts and plan our next adventure.

18

*Sailing the Leeward Islands—
Anguilla to Dominica*

We anchored for one last night in Virgin Gorda, in the British Virgin Islands, and then decided to sail to the island Anguilla, which is also British. We sailed overnight and found a great place to anchor in Aquarium Harbor, with beautiful beaches!

While we were in the US Virgins, we had made arrangements for Rena to fly into St. Martin for Christmas vacation and enrolled her in a ten-day scuba course.

We still had a week before we would arrive at the Simpson Lagoon, which is nestled in the Dutch side of St. Martin. We also invited the crew of another boat to spend Christmas and the New Year with us in St. Martin.

When we arrived in St. Martin, we checked in and went through customs, and all went well. Rena arrived safely, and we drove to the airport to meet her. She was ready for her new experience and had brought all her scuba equipment with her. She had passed her scuba course in Syracuse, but this would be much different.

When the course started, there were only three divers taking the course. The instructor was a young, good-looking guy. He explained that Rena would be transported to the class at 9:00 a.m. every morning and returned at 4:00 p.m., and lunch and assorted cold drinks would be provided on the boat. The plan was to do three dives a day, at different locations. After the first day, when Rena returned to our boat, she was happy and excited! We had dinner together, and then she went to bed, totally exhausted.

Cal was wise. He had thought, *If you want to keep a teenager out of trouble, keep her busy diving for ten days!* She loved every day and enjoyed the other teenagers. Having a very handsome diving instructor was a real plus!

Our friends Bob and Lee and their dog Chelsea were in the marina next to us. We spent so much time together and had great fun. We rented a car some days and toured the island. St. Martin has two areas, the French side and the Dutch side. We decided to have lobster and filet mignon for Christmas dinner, and I cooked for everyone. We also celebrated New Year's Eve with Bob and Lee and, of course, Chelsea. We had a wonderful dinner and drank champagne! At midnight there was a magical display of fireworks. It went on forever. I'll never forget that experience.

After ten days it was time for Rena to return home. She had received her scuba certificate and had a wonderful vacation. Now she was going back to her real life. She was studying music at a college in Hartford, Connecticut. She had brought her saxophone along and played for us several nights. She also blew in the New Year!

We drove her back to the airport. Surprisingly, she was very tanned but hadn't gotten sunburned. She was a redhead and usually burned easily. She had used plenty of sunblock, but being under the water most of the time must have made the difference.

After Rena left, our group went out to dinner to discuss where we would sail next. We needed a change of scenery.

Our next sail was to St. Barthelemy, a French island. Checking into customs was now an easy routine, and my ability to speak French helped a lot. Gustavia was the place to clear customs, and it was also a great place to anchor. After sailing all day, we were ready for a swim and a cocktail for sure!

The next day, we saw a boat anchored close to us. The boat was still flying its customs burgee. We decided to use our dinghy and make a visit. The couple had just arrived from England after making a long ocean crossing. They were so happy we spoke English. They told us they had tried to clear customs, but their passports had been withheld until customs officers returned to check their boat. We were still holding on to the side of their boat when the customs boat arrived. Along with the officers was a sniffing dog, looking for drugs. Thank God we were allowed to stay near their boat so I could act as the interpreter. The boat owner was a smoker who rolled his own cigarettes. Because of this, the officers suspected he was smoking something other than tobacco.

Anyway, the dog didn't find anything, their passports were returned, and the customs officers left. I was so happy I could help. My ability to speak many languages was very helpful throughout our travels.

The next day, we all had dinner together on our boat. We had a good laugh about the customs inspection. After that experience we were very careful as we sailed through the French islands. But there was always time for a little refreshment. I remember there being a great bar at the beach called Le Select—one of those little memories you never forget!

We were off once again, sailing to Barbuda, a British island. Nobody lived there, but we had great anchorage, and the beaches and snorkeling were superb. We stayed for about a week.

During our travels, Cal was reading a lot of books. We exchanged books with other boat owners, and every marina had a book exchange. I was able to find German books as well as books on so many different topics related to the local areas we traveled. I learned about the history of the islands, the fish, the birds, and all those particulars that made each island unique.

Then we ventured out to sail to St. Eustatius, a Dutch island. We found a five-star restaurant and treated ourselves to an elegant meal. Of course, we met with customs first. We were in and out of the island, then off to St. Christopher, a British island.

We always had to first meet with the customs agent. Once cleared, we teamed up with some sailing buddies. We found a tennis court, played, and enjoyed the activity! Each time you used the dinghy to go to town, you tipped a boy to look after the boat while you went shopping. We learned this was a very good practice if you wanted your dinghy to be there when you returned!

Every island had a different charm and unique character. Sometimes I'd find a fabric store, which made me very happy. I'd buy different fabrics on different islands for quilting, placemats, and any other projects I had in mind. I made cover-ups for us to wear after swimming when we relaxed on the boat. I became very creative after a while! I used my Bernina sewing machine all the time.

Now we were off to Nevis, another beautiful British island. We visited for a while, then continued on to the British island Antigua. We stayed in the English Harbour and rented a mooring ball. This was rented by the day. Once the boat was secured, we went off in our dinghy to explore the area. Every marina had a place for refuse and a location to do laundry. It was nice to be able to thoroughly wash sheets and towels. Part of my regular routine was to soak my wash in a bucket in the cockpit. I washed our clothes, then rinsed them in freshwater. Everything was then hung over the railings to dry in the sun. Everything dried very fast with all the sunshine. But there was nothing like having a washing machine do the job for you!

We had to care for the boat on a frequent schedule. Cal would wash and clean the boat inside and out. I would check for areas that needed more varnish. The deck was teak, but the handrails and the gunnels around the boat required periodic attention. This was my job, and I loved doing it. Anything that required painting was my project!

The next stop was the island Montserrat, also British. On our way there, we passed a big rock called the Kingdom of Redonda. A school of dolphins kept us company while we sailed to Montserrat.

You must wonder, how does one get exercise while sailing? Well, there's work to do on the boat, and we would swim and snorkel and sometimes play tennis. But I also did a regular exercise routine. I had a tape machine, and Jane Fonda was my workout partner—she kept me busy every day. We also had exercise mats so we could work out on the deck.

The freedom we felt from being on our boat was overwhelming and so much fun. We'd talk to our friends on the radio twice a day and decide where to meet up.

We all liked the dinghy drifts and watching the beautiful sunsets. We'd share knowledge about all the different rums that individual islands had to offer, a major part of our conversation when talking on the radio. We quickly learned which islands had the best-quality rums, and we all stocked up! Forget about wine or any other of your favorite poisons—rum was everywhere, the drink of choice, though some of it was so bad that I could have used it as my varnish remover.

We had learned earlier that Cal's parents and sister would be sailing into Montserrat on a cruise ship. We planned to have dinner with them. When the ship docked, we called to ask permission to board the ship. Permission was granted, and we went off with our dinghy to get to the cruise ship. Everybody was waving at us and cheering. We were able to spot Cal's parents and sister. Sitting in the dinghy next to the cruise ship made us feel very small! The crew put a long ladder down and helped us tie up the dinghy. Up the ladder we went! Of course, we had to be cleared through customs. We showed our passports to identify who we were. Once on board, we got a big applause from the people on the cruise ship!

After visiting Cal's parents and his sisters, we hugged each other—we still couldn't believe what we had done! We had a lot of stories to tell. We had such a great time. Then there was an announcement from the captain: the cruise ship had to leave because there was a storm coming!

We were on the cruise ship for only about one hour, and there was no time for our dinner plans. We had to get back to our dinghy and ride back to our boat. The crew helped us get to our dinghy. In the process, they gave us a big bag of fresh fruit, compliments of the captain. We boarded our dinghy, and the cruise ship prepared for departure. By the time we got back to our boat, the dinghy was nearly out of fuel, and it was 8:00 p.m. We watched the cruise ship pass our sailboat. We knew Cal's parents and sister were happy, and at least we'd had some time to visit. We only wished it could have been longer.

It was late, but we were hungry, so I started dinner. We decided to grill some steaks on the grill with a baked potato. We had lots of fresh fruit for dessert!

A storm was forecasted for the area, and that concerned us. However, we were anchored safely—or so we thought. We went to bed and fell asleep. Several hours later, I woke up and noticed that the boat felt different. We went on deck and discovered the wind blowing very hard. We were about three miles out to sea—our anchor had not held. We learned that Montserrat had black beaches as a result of volcanic activity over the years. The ocean floor in the area was not suitable for secure anchorage. The cruise ship had been anchored there before its departure but had left because the captain didn't trust the weather situation.

On our return trip back to shore, we noticed all the materials floating in the ocean. We had managed to pass through all of this during the night. We were so lucky that we hadn't hit any of it!

We spent time hanging out in Montserrat, then went off to Guadeloupe, a French island. Customs again! About five of our friends and their boats met us there. There was a big book exchange at this location.

I had learned how to cut my husband's hair, and Cal bragged about what a good job I did. Now I was being asked to cut hair! I became a barber and hairstylist! I once lined up about five guys on the beach, and they all got a Heidi haircut. You should have heard the conversation on the radio the next day. I ended up with many customers over the years. Of course, there was no charge. I had fun doing it. I bought a professional haircutting set in Syracuse and a pair of German left-handed scissors. The set included an electric shaver. I still have all the equipment just in case!

Dominica was the last of the Windward Islands, again a British island. We were always happy to be in a location where we could speak English. We visited here for a short time, and then we sailed to Forte Martinique, en route to Grenada.

Martinique was a great island for getting provisions. It had everything available, including good rum. We stayed in Forte de France, a superb place to visit. We all had an opportunity to shop, sightsee, and play tennis.

The time flies when you're on a boat; time means nothing. I called my mom whenever I could, but it wasn't possible for family to call us. Cal would joke around and say, "Ah, just let them find us." Half the time, I didn't know where we were. But having contact with Mom was important to me, and knowing Rena and Scott were doing well was my main priority when I called home.

When we knew we would be staying at a marina for a long period, we had our mail forwarded to the marina. I gave my mom the address right away and could hardly wait to get her letters. I always had several letters from my mom. Cal's sister forwarded all our other mail to us. Each time we got mail, it was like Christmas!

By this time, we had been sailing for about a year and were concerned about the upcoming hurricane season. We had to find a good place to hang out for the season. Many of our friends had decided to go to Grenada. On our way there, we went to the islands St. Vincent, Bequia, and Mustique, all of which had great anchorages. Then we passed Canouan and stopped again at Tobago Keys. At this point, only a few boats were traveling together. As we continued to Grenada, we passed a number of different islands, including the Union and Carriacou islands as well as Island de Ronde.

19

A Season in Grenada

Finally, we all arrived safe and sound in Grenada, a British island. When you approach the island, you can smell it. It is known as the Spice Island. We all anchored in St. George's Harbour, a protected bay. We knew this would be home for a while. Provisioning was great, and the island was beautiful.

We made this our hurricane escape place. It was great to be surrounded by many other boats. We were all friends and planned lots of shared activities. We planned dinner parties, played tennis, visited the town, and went for long walks. Of course, visiting all the spice factories and the coffee and chocolate plantations was a high priority. Grenada is the second-largest exporter of nutmeg and mace, the number one exporter being Indonesia. Mace is the yellow material that grows around the nutmeg.

One day while walking, I discovered a very beautiful trail. There was a very nice lady sitting under her mango tree. I introduced myself and told her I was so impressed by the beauty of the tree. She told me she had an abundance of fruit from the tree and suggested I help myself to some fruit and take it home. I thanked her and asked if I could pick the fruit on my way back from my walk. She said any time and any day was fine. I was so happy because I love mangos. I always had a backpack with me, so on my way back, I filled it with mangos.

While walking I also found a fabric store in St. George's Harbor, which delighted me. Cal found a place where we could haul the boat to have the bottom painted and other necessary repairs done.

Secret Harbor was located right in front of a beautiful resort owned by the Moorings. Our plan was to stay in the resort while our boat was out of the water being painted. Cal made reservations for the resort and the boat hall. It would be another month before we moved into the Moorings resort.

In the meantime, I was very busy finding ways to use the beautiful mangos. You could find me making mango jam and many other dishes with my new fruit. To this day I enjoy preparing one of my favorite recipes, chicken with mangos. Delicious!

Time flies by when you're having fun! The month passed quickly, and it was now time to lift the boat out of the water, pack our Caribbean 1500 bags, and taxi off to the resort. We had the most spectacular room with a balcony overlooking the harbor. We enjoyed the air conditioning for a while but actually found it to be a little too cold. We turned it way down and left the balcony door open—much better!

We played tennis every day and swam in the resort's tiled pool. From poolside, we could see all the boats anchored in the harbor. We often had our breakfast and dinner on the balcony in our room. The food was delicious, further enhanced by the beautiful views of the harbor. Many of our boating friends joined us for dinner, and needless to say, we had a great time!

One day, I chipped my tooth when I bit down on a very hard breadstick. We had to find a dentist. The resort manager recommended one, and I made an appointment and went to his office by taxi. The dentist was Dutch. He was competent and friendly and fixed my tooth without delay. To this day, I've never had another problem with that tooth.

The day came when the work on the boat was complete, and it was launched for us and ready for boarding. However, we decided to spend an extra night at the resort. We left the resort the next day and boarded the boat. In addition to painting the bottom, they had done the varnishing and cleaned everything. She looked great!

After many months, hurricane season was over. Cal's sister asked us to venture north to help out with his ailing parents. During our sail back to the British Virgin Islands, I discovered that my Austrian friends Hanni and Hugo were chartering a boat with a captain. We decided to get together. We went off in our dinghy to meet them and snorkeled in Monkey Bay together. It was a new experience for them. The pelicans dove into the water and were all around us. We watched them as they dove for fish. When we were done with the day's adventure, we anchored in Trellis Bay.

We got together one more time in Anegada and spent the day walking the beach and the evening dining on lobster. The next day, they left with their charter boat, and we were off to Bermuda! Bermuda, here we come!

20

Bermuda, Here We Come

It was late November 1993, and we were off to Bermuda. We found a perfect weather window and had a very pleasant crossing to our destination. We sailed about four days to get there. Cal, being a former military fighter pilot, contacted the military base to see if they had a buoy for us to use while in Bermuda. Indeed, they had one unused buoy for us so we could tie up our home, *Aries Won*.

There were so many exciting activities coming our way. The new location had tennis courts, an exercise facility (with a personal trainer), a fantastic swimming pool, a movie theater, and the only McDonald's on the island at that time. There was also a slot machine at the gas station that accepted American quarters.

We used our dinghy every day to explore all the little bays and beaches, which could be accessed only by small dinghies. It was a new experience for me to explore Bermuda this way. During our first crossing to Bermuda in 1992, all we had seen was the marina and Hamilton, the main town. There is so much more to this very special island. There are many small islands, some of them privately owned.

We saw white-tailed tropical birds with split tails thirty inches long and a wing spread of up to three feet. These birds were everywhere and were beautiful to watch with their graceful flying pattern.

Now it was almost Christmas, and Cal's sister wanted us to help out with their father, who had undergone surgery. We found someone to check our boat and do necessary repairs while we were gone. We trusted that the boat was in good hands and would be well cared for. There could be strong winds while we were away, and the buoy had to hold our forty-four-foot boat. We made our travel plans, cleaned the boat, and then flew to Syracuse, New York, wearing the only warm clothes we had with us.

It was nice to be back in our house for Christmas and to visit with family and friends. We had a lovely fire every night, making our home cozy and warm. We devoted our time to helping Cal's father recover from hip surgery. Rena was so happy to see us. The whole family celebrated Christmas together.

Syracuse can be very cold in the winter, so I was happy to wear the winter clothes we had waiting for us. We also managed to go skiing a few times.

After several weeks it was time to get back to Bermuda. We loved Bermuda so much, and the boat was in good condition when we returned. Staying in Bermuda for several months was heavenly! We decided to arrange for Rena and her friends to spend spring break with us in Bermuda. We took them on dinghy rides, and one night I had them all for dinner. A good time was had by all, but then it was time for them to return to school.

We had to get the boat ready to sail north. We shopped at the commissary for the last time and said our goodbyes to many new friends. After checking the weather (and also talking to Herb in Canada), we expected all would be okay for the trip north. Herb advised that there could be two lows in the weather pattern, but with some luck, that would not be a problem. Cal was thinking about that comment but was ready to go.

The dinghy was deflated and stored on deck again. We always followed the same safety procedures whenever sailing offshore. Everything was in place, and on the twenty-fifth of May, we were off! The weather was great, the sun was shining, and we were playing our favorite tape, "Sail Away"!

Given the forecast, the plan was not to exceed more than twenty-five to thirty knots. I didn't like the Gulf Stream and wished we had a third person with us for the watch shifts. But it was too late to think about that now. I had considered having my son Scott join us because he was a very good sailor, but he could not take time off from work.

21

Testing Our Survival Skills

The first night was calm, and a full moon led our way. The day of the twenty-sixth was pleasant but overcast, with strong winds. Cal saw some sharks swimming around the boat. He commented that he did not like the look of the sky. We contacted Herb to follow up on his latest weather report. He confirmed that the winds should not exceed more than thirty to thirty-five knots. We got the boat ready for the night. We had two reefs in the mainsail, furled the yankee, and put the staysail up. After supper the wind increased, but the autopilot could handle it just fine.

At seven the next morning, we had all the wind we could handle. One of the plastic sliders at the mast snapped. We brought down all the sails and motored. Cal had to hand-steer the boat running downwind with forty- to forty-five-foot seas and with winds up to forty knots and gusts up to fifty-five. What a roller-coaster ride! I felt I was in a washing machine. Cal was held down in the cockpit with two tethers so he would not get swept overboard.

Around 11:00 a.m., we lost one running backstay, and a few hours later, the other came crashing down. I tried but couldn't handle the wheel myself. I was nauseous, and all I could drink was hot tea and consommé, and I ate granola bars. It rained off and on all day. Cal was cold and tired, totally exhausted.

Twelve hours had passed, and we still had not reached the Gulf Stream. Now we were both in the cockpit, and things were beginning to calm down as the winds shifted. At this point we used our yankee and our Alpha 3000 and went on autopilot.

Cal contacted another boat and asked if we could get Herb's evening list to get a further weather update. We wanted to save our batteries for the autopilot.

Going through the worst weather, the boat had drifted about thirty-eight miles east, toward Halifax. Around 11:00 p.m. we tacked to get back on course. Cal could finally get some sleep—he was exhausted! The boat was now under control.

I was in the cockpit with both of my tethers on, the short and the longer one. I was secured and more stable in the cockpit. I was wearing my horseshoe collar and life preserver. I had my egg timer, some snacks, and a flashlight on hand for my watch duty, and I was wearing my waterproof wristwatch. We were pounding into fifteen- to twenty-foot waves. I had my egg timer on so I would not fall asleep. I had to keep watch for other boats passing through the area. The foul-weather gear kept me warm and dry. It was overcast and very dark, no moon and no stars. The waves had a lot of fluorescent sparkles, and I loved watching them.

I checked the time, and it was 1:00 a.m., Saturday, May 28. I felt the boat hit something in the water! We suddenly came to an abrupt stop. Thanks to my two lifelines, I was not knocked overboard. The impact was so great that I fell to the other side of the cockpit, the boat heeled sideways, and it felt like the boat came to a halt. The vibration was so overpowering. I was startled and frightened! First, we'd had the perfect storm, and now what?

I went below to see if Cal was okay. Cal was sitting up and yelled, "Heidi, get our stuff together! I think we're sinking!" When he stood, he was already up to his ankles in water.

Cal was soon starting the engine and working the bilge pump. We had to get the sails down. Cal lifted all the floorboards, checking for leaks from the seacocks and hoses, but we couldn't find the source of the leak. Where was the water coming from? We could not pump fast enough to control the incoming water.

The engine belt splashed water onto the alternator and fried it. Now we had no alternator. At 1:20 a.m. Cal made his first Mayday call. I sat down and made a list of important items that needed to be located and packed (insurance papers, passports, money, and jewelry, and I even packed my watercolor paintings).

A Falcon jet picked up our call on the radio and reported us to the Coast Guard. We were able to give them our exact location. I had gathered our things in double garbage bags that would be packed in the life raft.

Now the big moment came, and we had to launch our Givens life raft. How often do you do that! It was 3:30 a.m. Cal was now ready to pull the lifeboat cord. I worried that all wouldn't go well. I was thinking, *Life raft, please open!* I couldn't remember anybody testing the life raft. I knew that before we left Newport in 1992, everything had been tested and had been working fine. But this was for real, not a test. *Please open!*

Suddenly, it opened just the way it should. Cal never lost his sense of humor as he called out, "Here is home!"

The raft was tied to the boat, and it had a Velcro door that I had to jump into so I'd be secure in the raft. Cal assessed the situation for a while—timing was everything! He told me that when he said "jump," I had to jump immediately. The movement of the boat and raft had to be synchronized, with no room for error. I had to jump when they were both aligned. I jumped when Cal told me, and the Velcro door gave way, letting me fall inside the raft. Cal threw the bags to me, and luckily, I caught them.

Cal turned off the bilge pump and removed the batteries. We needed the batteries for the radio so we could stay in contact with the Coast Guard. We lowered another five gallons of water into the raft. We had all our emergency supplies, including one extra flashlight, all our flares, a bag full of military meals ready to eat, a first aid kit, and all our other emergency equipment.

Still on the boat, Cal was up to his knees in water. He changed the batteries to our portable VHF radio and GPS. We were thankful for Zipper bags—everything got to the life raft dry and ready to be used.

Now it was Cal who had to jump into the raft. He made the jump safely and finally used his Swiss knife to cut the raft loose from the boat. At this moment he said, "This is home—do you want to make whoopie?" I told him we were not in a James Bond life raft! Cal and his humor.

The Coast Guard was now in contact with us and asked us to shoot one of the flares. "Shit," Cal said. "Which side do I ignite? I don't have my reading glasses. If I light the wrong end, it could be a disaster!" He held the flare way outside the Velcro door and ignited the flare correctly. Boy, was I relieved when that went well!

There was a freighter from Finland in the area, and its crew saw our flare. By now it was about 4:00 a.m. The captain of the vessel, called the *Finnfighter*, contacted us on the radio and offered to rescue us.

As this big freighter inched toward our little life raft, the waves were still twenty feet high. It was too dangerous to climb those slippery metal ropes. I will never forget the noise of our life raft scraping along the side of the freighter. I thought we'd be ripped apart.

About 4:45 a.m., the Coast Guard helicopter had us in sight. We asked the *Finnfighter* to slowly back off and allow the Coast Guard to do the rescue. If we were rescued by the freighter, we'd have to go to Finland, the *Finnfighter*'s destination! The Coast Guard would rescue us and take us to the USA.

I readied myself for the rescue and lined up the garbage bags next to the Velcro door in order of their priority.

I looked up at the helicopter and saw a rescue swimmer/frogman (or whatever they are called) jump into the ocean from the basket that had been lowered. He swam as fast as he could to get to the life raft. When he got to the raft, he gave us both a nice smile and then looked at me and said, "Ladies first."

My life preserver was inflated, and the rescuer told me to hold on to him, and he would get us to the basket. I asked if I could bring some of my packed bags. He said my husband would be allowed to bring two bags on board. The swimmer again advised me not to do anything; he would get us to the basket.

I had my yellow rubber boots on, and they filled up with water, but he got me to the basket, which was slightly underwater. He told me to hold on, and with a big jerk and at rapid speed, I was lifted up in the basket. Two men pulled me into the helicopter.

I was one happy lady sitting on the helicopter floor. The swimmer went back to the raft to get Cal and two of the garbage bags. The swimmer then had to make a final swim back to the raft to sink it and discharge the auto signal. This would disengage the distress signal so that other ships would not attempt to do a rescue. The swimmer was then pulled up to safety, and off we went.

We learned that the rescue had lasted only eighteen minutes. To me it had seemed like a very long time. They were so nice to us. There was hot air available to dry our hair plus lots of warm blankets, hot chocolate, and some cookies!

The first thing I had to do was see if Cal had gotten the right bags off the raft. Hallelujah, yes, he had! We had all our important papers: passports, insurance papers, driver's licenses, credit cards, et cetera. We also had the jewelry, our money, and my little paintings. At 5:45 a.m., with daylight on the horizon, it was clear we were safe.

Thanks to Cal, we had never really panicked. It was an unbelievable adventure, one I hoped would never happen again!

We will never know for sure what we hit in the water. The Coast Guards thought, because of the very rough weather, that it was probably a container floating just under the surface. They also mentioned the possibility that it was the snorkel of a submarine.

This was rescue month, and we were the first rescue that month. A Falcon jet had been sent to get our position first, and its crew had filmed the whole rescue. The helicopter had arrived an hour later to bring us to safety.

After a two-hour flight, we arrived in Cape Cod, Massachusetts! The rescue had taken place about 300 miles offshore. The helicopter had had just enough fuel to bring us to Cape Cod. Fuel had been critical the whole time of the rescue. We were glad we hadn't known about the possibility of a fuel shortage. We learned this only after we landed.

Once we were on land, all we wanted was a nice hot shower! We had to borrow some Coast Guard jumpsuits because the clothing we had been wearing at the time of the rescue was all we had.

They gave us a hot breakfast, and we felt human again. We also got a short viewing of the rescue tape. I couldn't believe it. They had filmed the whole rescue, including our time floating next to the freighter. I could also see that our *Aries Won* was still afloat at that time. I hope the freighter picked her up and maybe made someone happy in Finland!

22

Back to Syracuse, 1994

We rented a car, and with our few belongings, we drove back to Syracuse. We still owned our home there, so Syracuse was our safe haven. After a long bubble bath and a change into fresh pajamas, we slept like never before.

We had our car in the garage, so we dropped off the rental car and resumed our usual routine. We did food shopping, called family and friends, and had very interesting discussions about the rescue film. Most people had read about the rescue or had seen it on television. It was fun to be home, surrounded by family and all of our things. It was still cold, so we enjoyed wearing all of our winter clothes.

Once we were settled, we contacted the Coast Guard and thanked them again for saving us, and we also returned the Coast Guard uniforms. Cal called the insurance company and learned that the company was in Chapter 7. Now what? We called the Coast Guard station and asked them to send a copy of the rescue film to the insurance company. The insurance company received the tape and within a few days finally agreed to give us the money for the price of the hull.

Because we had the tape and a report from the Coast Guard, we had evidence of the accident and rescue. The insurance company could not refuse our claim. What a great relief. We did not receive any reimbursement for the contents of the boat, which was a significant loss, but some recovery was definitely better than nothing.

We would be home for a while and thought it would be nice to see Mom. I asked her to visit us. I was so anxious to see her. She was happy to make the trip and traveled with a friend. We had such a great time. I had a party in her honor, and everyone had a good time. They stayed for two weeks.

Life in Syracuse was normalizing, and we were getting back to our usual routine: spending time with family and friends, playing tennis, and caring for Cal's parents. But something was missing!

One afternoon Cal and I were having lunch at the Syracuse Country Club. Cal looked at me and said, "I have a serious question for you: what would you think about buying another boat?"

I said, "What? Another boat?"

Well, we decided that we had fallen off the horse, and now we had to get back onto it. We planned to sell the house and put everything into storage, including our Jaguar. It was a new adventure and one that was very exciting for both of us!

We put the house on the market and started our search for our dream boat. It was not very long before we received an offer on the house. We told the buyers of our plan, and the family agreed to move to Syracuse only after we had found our new boat, our new home!

I started packing boxes for storage. I had a garage sale and was able to sell many things we would no longer need. We gave the children the things they wanted. It wasn't long before the house was emptied out. Now we had to find the perfect boat!

Cal wrote letters to boating friends and associates and looked at many boat advertisements. We traveled all over to look at boats. Then a phone call came from a boating friend. He told us he thought he had found us the perfect yacht!

He said, "The sellers are dear friends of mine who had the yacht custom-made for a sail around the world. It is a Tayana 52, a Bob Perry design." It came from the same designer as our Lafitte 44. The yacht was in Maryland, so off we went to take a look at her!

At the same time we contacted Steve Black, who was organizing another rally with the Caribbean 1500. This time they would sail from Virginia to St. Thomas. We were interested in participating in the race but first needed to find the perfect boat!

Well, we fell in love with the Tayana 52 and purchased our new home. Her name would be *Sojourner*! Our house in Syracuse was sold, and it was

Sojourn with Heidi

time to say goodbye. After getting everything in order, we said our final goodbyes to family and friends!

We learned that some of our friends who had done the rally with us last time were also participating in the upcoming race. We met up with the Brewers, Bob and Lee, who were sailing their yacht *Tai-Pan*. We sailed together and learned a lot about our new home, *Sojourner*.

One of Cal's fraternity brothers wanted to sail with us. He lived in Cape Cod and owned a schooner. I was so happy that we would have an experienced sailor on our next crossing. We sailed around Marblehead, and with the Brewers, we sailed to New York City. They gave us a great picture of *Sojourner* with the twin towers in the background. I gave them a picture of the *Tai-Pan* with the Statue of Liberty in the background.

We arranged to meet up with John, our crew member, on the way to Virginia.

Now in Norfolk, Virginia, we met many new people sailing the Caribbean 1500. The fleet had grown to sixty boats, all shapes and sizes. The owners of *Between the Sheets*, friends we had met back in 1992, were also taking the trip and helping Steve Black with the preparations for the journey.

Cal and I were asked to help with packing and organizing life rafts. We also offered a lecture on our sailing experiences with *Aries Won*.

Finally, after everyone was ready, on October 22, 1994, we set sail for St. Thomas, in the US Virgin Islands, in tandem with the Caribbean 1500. Many of the boaters and boats were first-time blue-water sailors.

We knew the routine from our previous crossing and quickly established a routine with regard to our watches. Our new boat was quite a bit faster and very stable. I did my best in the galley and loved to cook all my special meals. We arrived safe and sound in Crown Bay Marina four and a half days later. The Tayana 55, a bigger boat than ours, arrived a few hours ahead of us. But with our handicap (being a Tayana 52), after all the arrivals were tallied, our boat won the rally championship!

There were several parties organized by Arlene, who was working for Steve Black.

We knew Carol, the manager, and Barbara, who owned a travel agency in the marina. After a while folks started to head off to different destinations. We stayed a while with new friends and played tennis. In the evenings we enjoyed our dinghy drift rendezvous!

After sailing around the US Virgins for a few months to Culebrita and then St. Croix, St. John, and many of our favorite places, we were told that there was a phone call for Cal. So we sailed back to Crown Bay Marina and returned the phone call.

The phone call was from a California gentleman by the name of Alex Payne who made documentaries about rescues at sea. His program was called *Emergency Call*. He told us he'd like to fly to St. Thomas to interview us. He wanted to meet us and hear about our rescue and what had happened on our boat, what had happened to *Aries Won*!

About three days later, Alex Payne arrived in St. Thomas and interviewed us for his TV show. He got our permission to request the rescue footage from the Coast Guard and promised to send us the edited tape to be used for his TV program.

As of today, this was the best thing that could have been recorded about our rescue.

It has all the highlights of the rescue and the happy interview on our new boat *Sojourner* at Crown Bay Marina. The rescue tape is only fifteen minutes long and has been shown many times.

Our next excursion would be to Bonaire, a great diving area! Sailing there, we stopped at many of our favorite islands, including St. Lucia and Grenada. Then we sailed off to Trinidad and Tobago. We reconnected with our friends and explored the islands. The island people were so friendly, and we hated leaving this place.

Sojourn with Heidi

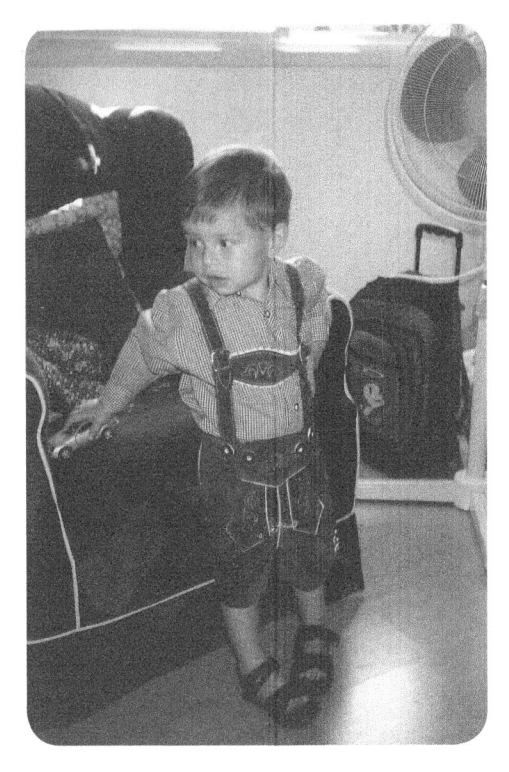

Grandchild, Victor, 2 years old, 2003.

I built a tennis court in Brazil, 2002.

Heidi Leitner Fearon

Scott and Renata got married, 1996.

23

Following the Wind

After a few days of sailing, we set course to Bonaire. Once there, we could not find a place with a secure anchorage. There was a very narrow shelf where we could anchor, and beyond that point the water dropped one hundred feet.

Later we thought we had found a secure location but then realized it was a designated swimming area for a hotel. I was so frustrated after this long and tedious search. I finally said to Cal, "Do whatever you want. I am going to bed." I did just that.

In the morning I asked, "Where are we?" Cal told me that we were almost to Curacao, a Dutch island. We discovered it was also a great place for diving.

We found an available buoy to tie onto and made ourselves a good breakfast. After breakfast Cal needed to get some sleep. We were now exploring the Lesser Antilles.

Curacao was a very nice place. There were horses available to ride along the beach. Typical of the islands, everyone was so friendly. The diving was spectacular, and the weather was clear and beautiful. We fell in love with the city and toured the impressive Dutch buildings. The architecture was similar to what you would see in Amsterdam. We ended up staying there for about three months.

There is one story I'd like to write about. I went to the marina laundromat to do my laundry. Just as I was about to start my first load, a lady came in with about five loads of laundry. I told her I wasn't in any rush, so she could use all the machines. By the time my husband came to get me, we had just finished doing all of her wash. I had spent a long time helping her with her wash and had not started doing ours.

Cal offered to drive the woman back to her boat. She was most appreciative. We helped her put her laundry into our dinghy, and off they went. There was only one surprise: when they got to her mooring, her boat was gone! All she had was clean laundry and a bag of coins for the washing machine and dryer. She was beside herself.

She spent the rest of the day and night with us. I made dinner for us on our boat. Now what? Her only explanation was that her boyfriend had taken off with another woman. She had some feelings about that.

The next day, Cal went to the US embassy to find out how to get her back home to the United States. Without a passport or anything else, this was not going to be an easy task. I don't remember the details, but she completed all the necessary paperwork, and other documents were sent to her from the US. She was able to fly home. Cal was kind enough to give her the money for her flight. Once she arrived home safely, she mailed us a check (care of the marina) covering all her expenses, with a very nice thank-you letter.

The things you experience living on a boat! Remember, when you go off to do laundry, bring your passport, credit card, and driver's license. Of course, you always hope to return to your mooring and find the boat there as well! We laughed about that experience for a very long time.

24

The Passing of My Mom

It was around this same time that I learned from my friend Veronica that my mom had passed away. I had tried to call Mom the prior two days, but she hadn't answered. I called Veronica to ask that she please check on Mom. Veronica had a key to Mom's house. Because of the phone service, Veronica couldn't get back to me, so I called her the next day and learned the sad news.

Veronica had found Mom sitting on the sofa with her food on a tray. She was wearing her favorite cashmere sweater, and the TV was playing. She loved watching *Dallas*.

In her typewriter was her last poem. Translated into English, it said,

"Now"

The soul is free, now she can fly
She can see the colorful world at her feet
With thousands of sparklers around her.
The happiness, the sky can reach her now ...

I already had a flight booked for Austria to surprise Mom and celebrate her ninety-second birthday. Her passing changed my life forever. I was so close to my mother.

In Austria, we had a celebration of her life following the cremation service. Many of her dear friends were there.

My brother said he would try to sell the house. I gave him Janet's address so that he could keep in contact with us, so that we'd know what was happening. I left with a very sad heart but had to get back to the boat. Cal was waiting for me.

25

Return to Cal and the Good Life

It was September 1995, and hurricane season was about to start. We decided, along with a group of friends, to pass the time in Venezuela.

After three months in Curacao, we left and found a few interesting islands en route to Puerto La Cruz. The small island Blanquilla was my favorite. The water was so clear, you could see hundreds of starfish. What a special sight. We were followed by a large school of dolphins performing for us.

One morning, a small local dinghy approached us and asked if we would give them some drinking water. Cal agreed, and they gave him the large empty plastic bottles that they had with them. They said for every bottle of water we gave them, they would give us a lobster. Our boat had a water maker, so we had no problem filling up their canisters. Lobsters, here we come!

We got so many lobsters. I boiled them for dinner and froze many of the tails for future feasts!

After visiting so many of the islands in the surrounding area, we decided to visit Venezuela and just relax. We would stay for months at the Maremares Marina. It was not easy to find the place. Plus, with a seven-foot draft, we had to inch our way to the dock with the help of a friend who guided us in his dinghy to our slot.

There were seven other boat friends from the Caribbean 1500 staying at the marina. We had our slot reserved and were the last boat to arrive. Many of our friends helped us get settled. They told us everything we needed to know about this heavenly place.

Maremares was a luxury marina. Every boat was assigned a room number, and we had all the same luxury services as other hotel guests. Each boat was given a doorbell and a portable air-conditioning unit that was installed over the main cabin hatch.

We were able to have meals served in our accommodations. The first night of our stay, we had a delicious meal served in the privacy of our own cabin. This was the height of luxury!

Besides a spa for massages and a huge exercise facility, tennis was also available (which we used every day). Most of our boating buddies played tennis. The pool was a wave pool. Every day an exercise class was available for guests. Because we could, we did it all!

Of course, golf was available, but at that time I didn't play golf. Twice a week there was a band, and everyone danced. There were some professional dancers available for dancing, so everyone had an opportunity to enjoy dancing! Cal was so happy about that because he knew I was a good dancer, and he loved to watch me dance. He always said he had two left feet when it came to dancing.

The resort had many great restaurants, and we frequented them often.

Leaving the premises was another story. The hotel had a shuttle bus to take guests into town. Puerto La Cruz was a busy city, and once in a while, a group of us traveled by resort bus to the shopping area. I was always happy when we returned.

We met some enjoyable people from one of the other boats and got to know each other very well. One gentleman was a professional bridge player. He noticed that all of the women in the group had ponytails. So he invented a card game for us and called it "ponytail canasta." It was played with six decks of cards. We had great fun playing this game every day. We played after exercise class, after the pool, anytime we could! The gift shop sold decks of cards, and the staff there told us they had never sold so many decks of cards! There were many people in our group, and all were buying at least six decks of cards for their boats. The basic canasta rules applied—there were four players, needing four canastas. However, the fun was the ponytail version. Whichever pair got the first canasta could pick up their pony, which was a pack of an extra eleven cards! I am still playing this game as of today.

Having found a very safe place for our boat, a group of us planned to explore Venezuela. Our first excursion was four days traveling to the Andes by bus. One night we all slept in hammocks. What an experience that was. We were close to the waterfall Canaima and could hear the water gushing all night. I was more afraid of snakes than anything else, but fortunately, that was not a problem.

The altitude was very high, so the views were breathtaking! All went well, but once the trip was over, we were happy to be back at the marina.

Then Cal decided to rent an airplane to explore Angel Falls. These are the longest falls in the world, so we had to see them.

We rented a car and drove to the local airport. The hotel had given us good instructions for how to get there. We found the perfect small private plane for our very exciting outing. Cal, of course, wanted to fly with me alone and explained that he had been a pilot in the military, but the owner said he had to fly with us. Cal would be the copilot and take over when instructed to do so.

All we needed was our American Express card, and off we went. I was in the back seat, ready with my camera. Ultimately, we were pleased that the owner of the airplane was with us. He spoke the language and knew how to get to Angel Falls.

When we arrived and saw the falls, we were stunned by their beauty. Now it was Cal's turn to fly. He flew up and down the falls, over the top and down again. My camera was very busy, and I have many pictures of that great day! The owner flew us back to the little airport and congratulated Cal on his flying skills.

There are many smaller waterfalls around the area. We decided to take another bus trip to the falls, organized by the hotel. Well, everything went wrong that day. We were served awful food, and then on the way back to the hotel, the car broke down.

Somehow, we managed to get a taxi to get back home. All twelve of us on tour decided this would be our last waterfall trip in Venezuela.

Maremares, Venezuela, was like Shangri-La. I wanted to stay forever. But hurricane season was over, and we all knew we had to move on soon.

Scott and Renata married in Canada on June 14, 1996. I could not be there. But there was a second reception in Brazil on December 6. I would be there! I found a linen dress for the occasion and planned the trip to Brazil. I traveled alone because Cal was visiting his daughter in Australia during this same time.

This was my first trip to Belo Horizonte in Brazil. Renata's parents had a beautiful home with a pool and a tennis court. The reception was set up in the four-car garage and included the tennis court area. The Catholic church service was lovely. A band played music throughout the day and night.

What I found very different was how the ladies prepared for the day. Renata's two sisters, her mother, and I all went to a salon to have a professional apply our makeup and style our hair. When I looked in the mirror afterward, I didn't recognize myself. *What have they done to me?* I thought. My hair was pulled back, and the makeup—oh my God! When I look at the pictures now, I hate them. Before the evening party started, I grabbed my hairbrush and combed my hair the way I liked it. I must have had about twenty pins in my hair!

The dinner was excellent, and the music played until three in the morning. Everyone was dancing, including me. There must have been about 150 people at the reception. It was an elegant, festive Brazilian affair.

After the wedding, I immediately returned to Venezuela. Some boats had already left. Four of us remained and would soon be leaving for new adventures. The hotel staff were very helpful and guided us out of the area with a dinghy. It was high tide when we left, but still we touched bottom twice with our seven-foot draft. We literally inched our way out of the area, the same way we had come in. I had bought lots of filet mignon to enjoy while we traveled. Beef was very inexpensive in Venezuela. Cal played our favorite tape, "Sail Away," as we sailed away to new horizons!

The first stop after Puerto La Cruz was Los Roques. These islands were still in Venezuela, but we had already checked out of the country. The water was crystal clear, and I felt like swimming in the ocean.

Here we went again, just the two of us planning another offshore sailing trip.

We had our charts out and decided to sail directly to St. Thomas in the US Virgin Islands, about 555 miles away. This would be a three- to four-day sail. All went well!

When we were about two days out to sea, a Coast Guard boat checked on us. We reported that all was well. They knew that we had checked out of Venezuela. We felt very comfortable with the Coast Guard watching over us as well as our friends.

26

The US Virgins (Islands!)

St. Thomas was warm and friendly, as always. Carol, the marina manager, had a dock ready for our arrival. A few hours later, another sailboat docked next to us, and we helped the man with his lines, although he was prepared to work them himself. The man captaining the boat was none other than Walter Cronkite. Cal recognized him as the well-known reporter and journalist.

"Yes, I am Walter," he said. Over the next few days, we got to know him—what a great man!

Some of our boat buddies wanted to spend some time in Culebrita. We all met there and had the time of our lives.

People asked us many times, "What do you do all day long?" What a silly question. Among other things, I used my new Pfaff sewing machine for various projects, like sewing a new mattress cover and making new living room cushions. I was sewing a lot. I was also painting, knitting, and enjoying myself varnishing the boat (boat care was again an ongoing activity). In addition, I read a lot; there were so many great books. Because we spent much of our time socializing with friends, I was often visiting my cookbooks and preparing for dinner parties and dinghy drifts. Our physical activities included snorkeling, hiking, tennis, and golf. But sometimes we just relaxed, reserving time to admire beautiful sunrises and sunsets. What a way to pass the time of day and night.

Living on a boat means there is always work to be done. As with *Aries Won*, my husband did all the cleaning, and I did the cooking and laundry. I also still loved the varnishing. Cal could fix almost anything. When he wasn't working on our boat, he often helped other boaters in the group. We kept a wide variety of spare parts in a locker because you never knew what might break down.

Now it was time to sail to Puerto Rico's main island! First, we stayed in the military marina, Roosevelt Roads. There we made use of the officers' club and the commissary. We then rented a car and explored Puerto Rico.

Cal had helped a very nice man in Culebrita fix something on his boat. As a thank you, he had offered us the use of his dock at his Puerto Rico home. He would not be using the dock because he planned to be away for three months. I had written down the address and hoped we'd be able to take advantage of his offer. With a very good map, we found our way to his place. The dock could hold an eighty-foot boat. The gentleman owned a fifty-five-foot power boat.

The magnificence of the home was equal to that of his lovely boat. I would say this beautiful three-story home must have been worth in the millions. Across from the dock was the most beautiful swimming pool. What an extraordinary place to offer to a stranger.

There was a maid working at the house. She had been told that we might be tying up at the dock. She showed us around and guided us to the water hose and the power plug. "And yes, please use the pool," she said. "Don't worry about the pool service. They come once a week." Well, this was another night to celebrate!

It was a very short dinghy ride to a spectacular beach and a casino. I thought I had died and gone to heaven. I called a friend in Syracuse and invited her to come to Puerto Rico to visit with us. She did visit. We had a wonderful time.

We stayed at this glorious facility for about two months. We had massages at a spa, and I discovered a great hairdresser and nail salon. Life doesn't get much better!

As wonderful as it was, the time came to move on. What would be next? We knew we'd be heading north again. In our travels we had met a very nice couple who also sailed with the Caribbean 1500. They had a house on Block Island. The wife was also a great artist. We had often painted together while sitting on the beach.

We had learned that sailing the Bahamas was not a good idea. Having a seven-foot draft was a challenge, not easy sailing. The decision was made:

we would make our way to see our friends on Block Island in Rhode Island. The weather window was perfect! Off we went, just the two of us.

About two days out to sea, we encountered a strange sight. A helicopter went very low and dropped a parcel in the ocean. We looked at the chart and saw that there was a shoal about ten feet deep in that area. Shortly after, a very fast power boat (a cigarette boat) came to the drop location. A diver on the boat dove into the water and came back up with the package. The parcel had a floating buoy attached, so it had been easy to locate.

Cal's immediate concern was that we were seeing a dope drop. The people on the boat knew we were close enough to spot them. We could have reported the incident to the Coast Guard, but because anyone could listen in on radio conversations, we did not make contact and pretended not to have seen anything. We realized we were in a dangerous situation. Sailing out there alone was not a good idea. We were afraid for our lives and sailed on.

Block Island is situated between Long Island and Martha's Vineyard. Getting there was a long and beautiful sail well worth the trip. We anchored at a perfect spot and rested up after many days at sea. We launched our dinghy and went ashore to call our friends (cell phones didn't exist then). Our friends were home and drove to the dock to meet us.

We had dinner at their home and talked about all our experiences. We loved Block Island. My friend and I signed up for a painting workshop.

I had a new friend in the water who began greeting us every day. It was a very friendly seal. What a special creature. We fed him only once, and that was that. He wanted more. When you spot seals, you know the water is cold.

After many weeks at Block Island and after finishing the workshop, we had to say goodbye.

We were off to a lovely marina in Mystic, Connecticut. We docked near the marina, within walking distance of lots of restaurants. We selected a restaurant where we had dined two years earlier because I remembered dinner there being very good. After dinner, the manager came over to greet us.

I said, "I have a question. About two years ago, we dined here, and I left my camera hanging on the back of my chair. Did someone find it?"

The manager asked me to go with him to the lost and found box, and there was my camera! I couldn't believe it!

Sojourn with Heidi

I said, "Cal, look what I found." My name was written on the camera case.

The next day, I found a camera shop and had the film developed, and there were all the pictures of our trip. It was so much fun to see the pictures and reminisce about the trip. An Asian family had found the camera at their table. They had finished the film during their meal at the restaurant, so there they were also on film. I wish I could say thank you!

Months later, we decided again to sail with the Caribbean 1500 from Norfolk, Virginia, to St. Thomas. Our friends from Block Island would also be making the trip. Now we were old-timers, seasoned sailors! We helped out as much as we could. We took a crew with us this trip and successfully completed the sail again.

Crown Bay Marina at that time was like home to us. We met many old friends in the bar and restaurant called Tickles. Yes, we had to have a Bushwhacker. Our crew flew back to the United States, and we were free to do whatever. And whatever we did. Hooking up with lots of our favorite friends, we visited all our favorite places.

Cal and I decided to spend the hurricane season in Venezuela just one more time. We'd be at the marina and hotel Maremares. It was hurricane season 1997, and arriving at Maremares was again like coming home. Many of our friends were there and already playing our ponytail canasta. Life was good. I had a birthday coming up, and without my knowledge Cal planned a surprise for me.

I could see the hotel staff putting tables and chairs on the marina deck and setting out tablecloths. I was below in my boat, sewing one of my projects. All of a sudden, my boat doorbell rang. When I peeked out into the cockpit, about forty people from the marina sang "Happy Birthday" to me. I was in tears and couldn't believe it. What a surprise Cal had planned for me. There was a beautiful huge birthday cake with "Happy Birthday, Heidi" written on it. There was food for everyone and a huge bucket filled with champagne bottles. The celebration went on all afternoon, and the band played through the night. We danced under a full moon. I will never forget that surprise birthday as long as I live. Someone taped the party, and I have played the tape many times.

Having enjoyed many years of sailing and many years of exploring, in 1997 we went one last time to the US and joined the Caribbean 1500 for the third time!

27

Concerns regarding Cal's Health

While we were in Puerto Rico in the Virgin Islands, Cal had a physical examination at the military hospital. They said his heart was a bit enlarged, but everything seemed to be okay. We had lunch at the officers' club, and Cal invited all our boat buddies to join us for lunch.

Again the question was asked, "Do we sail north or south?" At times Cal felt a bit tired, and I was worried about him. He said, "All is good. Let's go one more time to Venezuela."

"Okay, you know we love it there," I said.

When the time was right, we sailed back to Maremares. The crossing was very tiring for me. Cal was exhausted all the time, and I had to do most of the sailing.

I asked Cal to be with me in the cockpit so that if I needed some help, he would be right there. Somehow we made it to the island Blanquilla, but we were both exhausted. I think we slept two days to recover from that journey.

We were pleased to be at the marina and began settling in with our friends. We seemed to be getting back to normal. We were playing tennis again with our friends, for example. However, some days Cal would suggest I play without him. He said he'd play another day. It was unusual for him not to play because we loved playing together.

We were both tired, although his tiredness was coming on more often. I had to convince Cal to see a doctor. One of our sailing friends was a physician and found that Cal had a low-grade fever. "There is no way I will go to a physician in Venezuela," Cal told me, and that was that! We planned to fly out of Caracas to Hilton Head.

It was now June 1998. We learned that Cal's father had passed away in February 1998, at ninety-seven years old. He had a long and full life and played golf most of his life. Golf was one of the main reasons he had built a house on Hilton Head Island in Sea Pines. Now that Cal's father had passed away, we planned for Cal to go to the military hospital for a checkup.

Cal was very tired, but that was his only complaint. Our duffel bag was stuffed with our traveling clothes. We lined up at the American Airlines counter, checked in, and got our boarding passes. No sooner did I get the boarding passes in my hand than someone snatched them from me and ran off. Cal was sitting down, and I had to do something. Security did nothing!

I ran after the man and caught him and asked, "What do you want?"

"Money," he said.

I happened to have a hundred-dollar bill with me. I gave him the money and felt lucky to get our passports and boarding passes back. I thought I was having a heart attack!

After going through security and finally getting to our seats, I said, "Someone up there was helping us."

28

Cal's Diagnosis Is Confirmed— Finding a Home on Hilton Head

The flight to Hilton Head went well. It was July 6, 1998. Janet, Cal's sister, and her husband were in Hilton Head. We settled in at Cal's parents' house as we prepared for Cal's medical appointment at the navy hospital in Beaufort. Cal's mother had Alzheimer's disease and was residing in a facility near Syracuse.

The navy hospital was where we got the bad news. Following a CT scan, the physician reviewed the report and told Cal he had cancer. Cal walked out of the physician's office and gave me the thumbs-down. I knew then it was bad news.

The day before we learned the news, we had celebrated Janet's birthday. She had then left the day of Cal's appointment to get back to her home in Cazenovia. Janet didn't learn the news about her only brother until after she had left.

It was cancer of the pancreas, and it had spread to the liver. I was devastated and couldn't stop crying. The doctor scheduled a needle biopsy for Wednesday, July 15, at seven thirty.

Bad news travels fast! Soon all our boat friends, children, and family had called and wished us the best. They knew it was a very difficult situation for us. Everything was happening so fast.

We would be staying in Hilton Head, and Cal would be followed by Dr. Thomas, an oncologist at Hilton Head Hospital. The hospital was an easy drive and convenient for the family. Cal was still a very strong man.

He got tired easily but still did all that he could under the circumstances. Sometimes I wish I hadn't pushed him so hard. I am so sorry!

Rena, Jason, Beth, and Scarlett came for a visit. It was very tiring for Cal. After telling them very gently not to get mad, he explained that he needed to rest and asked them to leave. There were lots of tears, all the time. I thought I was cracking up.

On Monday, July 13, Debbie came from Australia to see her dad. I gave them some time alone and went off with a realtor to see some properties. Cal's father's estate had not been settled as yet, and Cal wanted to find a house for us. I had always liked Hilton Head, and Cal thought it would be a safe place for me to live.

We went for lunch at the Boathouse with Debbie. I couldn't eat a thing. It must have been my nerves.

Christeen, a German realtor, called to say she might have found the right place for us. Cal wanted his own place and wanted all our stuff brought from storage in Syracuse.

The next day was the big day for the needle biopsy. Cal had a nap and was shivering. Even with all the blankets, he was still cold.

While in the hospital, he saw a lady behind a window putting a cigarette down. Cal opened the sliding window and told her to stop smoking because it would kill her. Cal never smoked! This was the kind of humor he had. Then he came out wearing the hospital gown and asked, "How do you put this on?" It was a wrap style.

Well, the biopsy confirmed that Cal had cancer of the pancreas. It was a fact. I had to accept it.

Looking for the right house for us kept me busy. Janet and her husband came back to visit, so we had them as well as Debbie staying with us. Cal wanted to find a house in Hilton Head Plantation, or HHP. The HHP rules did not allow short-term rentals, the community was closer to the bridge for any evacuation, and it was higher ground from the ocean. He didn't want waterfront property but did want a pool. We wanted our home to be on one level and have a two-car garage.

Christeen wanted me to look at a place she thought was just right for us. I looked at the house and loved it! Now I had to get Cal to see the place.

After Cal's first chemotherapy treatment, Christeen came for us, and we went to see the house. Cal said, "I don't see anything wrong with it," and he asked me if I liked it. I said yes.

Christeen told us that someone had already made an offer. Cal told her that he would pay the full asking price. He wanted the house, and that was that. After filling out all the paperwork, Cal wrote a check, and that was the beginning of owning our new house! By the way, twenty-one years later, I am still in the same house and loving it.

Two days later, we moved into the house. We had a king-size bed in the master bedroom, a few wine glasses in the kitchen, and a glass dining table with six chairs. I went out and bought two pillows, some sheets, a quilt, towels for our bathroom, and other necessities we needed. We were so happy to have our own place.

The worry about Cal was unbelievable. We relaxed in our new hot tub and pool. Cal did whatever he could to make sure I was comfortable. We got all our belongings from storage, and slowly everything fell into place.

Bill Ruth, a local lawyer, settled the will and paperwork. Janet drove our Jaguar from the storage area to Hilton Head. We had a car again! I bought a cheap sewing machine and started to sew curtains. All was going fine with the house, but Cal was getting weaker every day. It wouldn't be long.

29

Cal's Passing—September 24, 1998

The dreaded day came. Cal passed, and I had to cope. I had lots of things to do. I had hung our bedroom curtains the day before Cal passed away. It was almost like he had been waiting for the curtains to be finished.

Before he passed, Cal had arranged for everything that I would need. He had made sure I had an exterminator, a pool service, a landscaper, and a cleaning service.

To fill up my days, I joined everything, and I volunteered too. I was ushering at concerts and plays. I was already a member of the tennis club. I joined the Art League. I also signed up for workshops and joined the photographers' club. Keeping busy was the only way I could deal with my loss.

A couple of months after Cal died, our friends brought our boat from Venezuela to Savannah, arriving on Thanksgiving. A lot of things had gotten damaged, especially with the sail. The jib was torn, and the refrigerator didn't work. The boat was a mess, and I had my work cut out for me.

Thanks to Bob and Lee, at high tide we carefully motored the boat into Windmill Harbor. I rented a slip from a dock owner, next to the clubhouse.

Now my work on the boat would begin. Bob and Lee helped me with everything.

They lived in the May River Plantation, about twenty minutes away, and spent so much time with me. Every day, I unloaded boxes of items off the boat. I had many boxes, so I made a list noting the contents of each one, so that there would be no confusion. It was all very well organized.

We had so many spare boat parts for the heads, the engine, the refrigerator, and so on. We also had extra sails and a complete set of new sails in storage. All of the items were boxed, labeled, and added to the list.

In the process of cleaning, boxing materials, and maintaining the boat, I had the jib and refrigerator repaired. By the time we were finished, I had moved twenty-nine full boxes from the boat to my garage. Included were two full boxes of tools! I cleaned everything and hired a young gentleman to clean the boat every week and check the hull for barnacle growth.

The only things remaining on the boat were my tapes (so I could play music), wine glasses, and some wine and rum. I didn't cook on the boat, but I had my refrigerator working, so I had plenty of ice.

I had use of the yacht club and played tennis at Windmill Harbor. I was so busy that the time passed very quickly. I was enjoying my new tennis friends, and life was beginning to normalize. I was beginning to heal. Lynn helped me a lot, on and off the tennis court. We are still best friends.

I had so much mail from family and friends that still needed my attention. After Christmas, I replied to everyone and thanked them for their support. Here is the letter I wrote to all of my friends and family in January 1999:

My dear … … … … … …

It is still very hard for me to answer your kind letter. Cal will be with me always. I still can't believe he's gone.

This poem was read at the service in Oneida, NY. The words were as if Cal had spoken them himself. It was titled "Miss Me But Let Me Go."

He was a hero to the very end, when he said to me: "Heidi, I am going fast. You will see that I am right." (Being right was a very important part of his life; he was not wrong very often.) I wish he could have been wrong this time.

Cal told it as it was. He was not the greatest charmer, but he was a truthful man. He had nothing to prove to anyone—he had done it all!

I am so thankful that we had such wonderful, eventful, and exciting years together. We did so much in a relatively short time, but it seemed like a lifetime!

I sure hope I gave Cal the best years of his life. Living together on two boats, the Lafitte 44 and the Tayana 52, for six and a half years, brings you very close together. This only works if you love and respect each other and become a real team. It also helps if you don't get seasick!

At the very end Cal said, "I have done it all. Sailing the ocean was the only thing missing, and we have done that too. My time has come to make room for someone else." Cal knew that his daughter Debbie was expecting a baby.

With all the friends we made together, our sailing buddies were like family to us. They are the greatest bunch of all! The many letters, flowers, phone calls, gifts, funny cards, and jokes we received were overwhelming. You all made Cal smile so many times, and he appreciated and loved it. I still don't know how to thank you for giving so much.

Because of you, our sailing friends, Sojourner is now in Hilton Head at a very safe marina and dock. She rests in Windmill Harbor! This is just minutes from our house. I am sorry to say that the Sojourner has to be sold. My cruising days have ended, but that does not mean I will never sail again. That time of my life will always belong to Cal, my Schatzi and love.

I am slowly coping to be on my own and managing this new life.

I spent Christmas and New Year's with Scott and Renata in Brazil. Renata's big family and many parties were a great break from everything. The weather was perfect, and we all had fun.

Now back in Hilton Head, mail and phone messages were waiting, and I'll be back to my new life—playing tennis, riding my bike, painting, and doing a lot to keep me busy. It helps me to cope. Evenings and nights are still very hard for me. Everyone says that with time it will get better. Cal wanted me to paint, and I am doing that and love it.

I am strong but also weak at times. I know without you I would not have coped the way I am right now.

Wishing you all the best for the year 1999, and thank you very much again for all the help and support you have given us.

Please stay in touch.

With love ...

30

Getting the Boat Ready for Sale

With my boat at Windmill Harbor, I spent most of my time getting the boat ready for sale. I played tennis at Windmill Harbor so I could be close to my boat.

In preparation for the sale, I cleaned everything and washed all the storage compartments. Then I painted the inside of them. After that was done, I cleaned and waxed the teak floors and cabinet doors. It took me a long time to do it all. Many nights, I slept on the boat.

My Austrian friends Hanni and Hugo First asked if they could visit me in Hilton Head. Of course, they could. I was looking forward to seeing them.

I was just finishing my last job on the boat when I decided to lift my floorboards up around the mast to clean the water and grime out of the bilge. I had a cup of coffee at my side and said to myself, *I have done it!*

However, my eye went in the direction of a string hanging from the mast. *What is this?* I wondered. Of course, I had to pull the string. Oh my God, it was a tampon! The previous owner had put it there, causing the mast to fill with water—and of course, the purpose of the open area was to allow water from the mast to drain into the bilge. Once the tampon string was pulled away, water gushed out at me and into the bilge.

I had to laugh. I remembered Cal telling me many times that the boat was not pointing right. He was right again. The mast had been filled with water, all sixty-five feet of it. And I had thought I was finished! After cleaning up the mess, I said, "What a great advertisement for a tampon!"

When all was really finished, I bought myself some flowers for the boat and celebrated with a nice rum cocktail. I bought a small "For Sale" sign and placed it on the bow. I never heard from my broker, nor did I ever see the boat advertised.

My friends from Austria arrived, and we had a great time riding bikes, spending time on the beach, visiting Savannah, and playing ponytail canasta some evenings.

My next visitor from Austria was Veronica and her friend. We did much of the same but played a lot of tennis as well.

Then Horst and Friedegard arrived in Hilton Head. We spent our time playing a lot of tennis and cooking and grilling. Friedegard is a superb cook. I learned again how to make the perfect apple strudel!

Time flies! Around Christmastime, my friends Aki and Minako visited from Montreal, and I had a Christmas party. I had Gimbeld candles in the dining room near my Christmas tree. As the guests were leaving, I realized a candle had fallen onto the Christmas tree and started to burn it. Aki very quickly unplugged the tree and got the kettle, which was always filled with water. He was able to extinguish the fire. After that I never lit those candles again.

The *Sojourner* had been residing at Windmill Harbor for a year. The contract for the broker had ended. I didn't call to extend the contract.

Pal, a staff person at Windmill Harbor, did a great job cleaning the outside of the boat and also did the varnishing. He was interested in knowing the kind of paint I had used on the hull—he was amazed that nothing was growing on it. I decided it must be the paint that had been used when the boat was overhauled in Puerto Rico.

31

A Very Special Day—A Buyer for the Boat

I had just gotten off the tennis court in Windmill Harbor. I was getting into my boat, preparing to get comfortable in the cockpit, when I noticed a nice gentleman looking at the boat. He asked if he could look at it. I hesitated and said, "Only if you're seriously interested."

He immediately wrote me a big check and handed it to me. "Well," I said, "you must be serious." I asked him to come on board. I was impressed because he took off his shoes before getting inside the boat.

The boat looked great! I always had flowers on the table. The man's name was Pete, and he wasn't saying much, but I could tell he liked what he saw. Finally, he said, "Heidi, can I come back tomorrow with my wife and get the tour?"

We established a time, and Julie and Pete arrived the next day to look at the boat again. They were very interested and asked for a sea trial. I agreed and told them I'd call him with the date.

Now I needed Bob and Lee to help me with the sea trial. What great friends to have! We set a date and time. I had to check the tides because with a seven-foot draft, the boat needed to leave Windmill Harbor with the high tide. We all wore our khaki shorts and white T-shirts—a great-looking uniform!

Windmill Harbor had a lock, so we needed to call the dock master to open it. This was the first time the sails had gone up since the *Sojourner* arrived at Windmill Harbor. Lee was at the helm, and Bob and I worked the sails. We had to tack very often, but we knew the procedure. I hadn't forgotten how to sail! Everything went smoothly. After the sails were put away and we furled the jib, we were on our way back to our dock.

Pete and Julie wanted the boat. The two best moments of owning a boat are first when you buy it and second when you sell it. The next step, after establishing a reasonable price, was lifting the boat out of the water to examine the hull.

Pal was right: nothing was attached to the hull. The boat had a very clean bottom.

The boat was hauled to the Palmetto Bay Marina. This was also where she would stay because Pete and Julie had rented a dock there for the boat. It was a happy and sad time. I had to sell her, but I would miss her a lot.

Then something terrible happened. The broker found out about the sale and wanted his commission. A boating friend had gotten Cal this broker, but he had never shown the boat to anyone. Also, his contract had ended. Now I had to get a lawyer to help me out.

The broker knew my status as a recent widow and had decided to take advantage of my situation. He fought to the bitter end. I also didn't hire the right lawyer because I still had to pay. I paid the fee and felt very much alone. I didn't have nice thoughts about this crooked broker.

Ruth came to visit me from New York. I was able to show her the boat because she was still at Palmetto Bay Marina.

The funniest thing was when I told Pete and Julie that everything belonging to *Sojourner* was waiting for them in my garage. They knew I had a brand-new set of sails but didn't know about the many boxes of spare parts, tools, and so on. My garage felt very empty after the boxes were removed!

Sojourn with Heidi

Selling Sojourner, 1989.

And then there was Al, 1995.

32

My New Life on Hilton Head as a Bachelorette

The year 2000 had come and gone. My grandson Victor was born in 2001. Scott and Renata were living in Brazil at the time. Renata had endured several miscarriages before having Victor and was extremely happy to have a healthy, happy baby boy.

Every year, I spent time in Brazil and watched Victor grow from an infant to a young boy. He was taking swimming lessons, and at six years old, he started playing tennis.

Renata's family had a big farm with a beautiful house and a separate party building. There was also a playground, a soccer field, and a badminton court. The farm had a variety of animals, including dogs, horses, cows, pigs, and chickens. There were servant quarters, and the staff looked after everything. The family had a cleaning staff and a cook who looked after a huge vegetable garden.

I thought, *Only one thing is missing: a tennis court.* Well, I broke down, and for Scott's birthday we built the tennis court. After it was completed, I traveled to Brazil to see it. What a great court. It was made with red clay, which was similar to the area's natural soil. The lines were a white brick used specifically for tennis courts. A practice wall was also part of the complex. It was all very special!

We had a sign attached to the fence and named the area "The Heidi-Ho Tennis Court." Scott and I had to play an exhibition match, and the whole family watched.

33

The Hilton Head Island Experience

I was adjusting to my new life in Hilton Head. I began working at the Port Royal tennis pro shop six hours a week. I worked weekends and loved it. Weekends were still a difficult time for me. Working at the pro shop brought me back to fashion and clothing. It was just what I needed at the time. Needless to say, the little money I made was invested in tennis clothes. I played tennis Saturday mornings from 8:30 to 10:30 a.m. and then went to work from 12:00 p.m. until 3:00 p.m. Sundays, I worked from 12:00 p.m. until 3:00 p.m. but played no tennis.

It was around this same time that I started to think about playing golf. One of the advantages of working at a pro shop was free tennis and golf! I started taking golf lessons and was told I should play right-handed. I am left-handed with everything except for writing. I was forced to write with my right hand in school. This went on for some time, but it never felt natural.

I also volunteered for our local golf tournament as a Shotlink volunteer. I had to measure the distance of the drives with a machine designated for that purpose. I liked doing it.

I was trying so many new things. In September 2003, I had my own exhibition with the Art League at Pineland Station. The exhibit was called "Sojourn with Heidi." My son Scott and all my friends came to the event. The exhibit was a success, and I sold all of my thirty-six watercolor paintings. What a special month.

In February 2004, two of my sailing buddies, Tom and Gina, and I planned to charter a boat in the Virgin Islands. I would take the last little box of Cal's ashes with me and spread them over the ocean at Lameshur Bay. This had been Cal's wish, and I would be able to finalize his last wish.

There happened to be people on another boat whom we knew from the Caribbean 1500. So we gathered petals from some flowers onshore and went out on the dinghy with Cal's ashes and had a very special ceremony.

Right after the Caribbean trip, I went skiing. I now belonged to the Hilton Head Island Ski Club. We took trips every year, mostly in the USA. Every year, we went to a different location. Our trips outside of the United States included Banff, Alberta, in Canada. I love my skiing buddies and was so happy to be skiing again.

During this time I was still driving my Jaguar. I was going out for dinner with friends and enjoying all that Hilton Head had to offer. I did have one unfortunate event: someone stole my golf clubs out of my car. I had to lock the trunk of the car with a key, and sometimes I forgot to lock it.

One of the best things I did was join the country club. The very first time I worked with the golf pro there, he threw a golf ball to me, and I caught it with my left hand. He said, "You are a left-handed golfer." I developed a whole new feeling for the game. I got myself a left-handed golf set and attended the six-month Golf Academy on Hilton Head. I had a hard time at the beginning, but it was much more natural for me to play left-handed.

In May 2010 I received some very sad news. After many years of suffering with multiple myeloma, Janet, Cal's sister, passed away on May 11. What a sad day for the whole family in Cazenovia, New York.

After that tragedy I did some traveling. I visited an island close to Rio de Janeiro called Ilha de Comandatuba.

I have never seen such luxury. Victor was about six years old. The children were picked up by a small train and spent the days together. Each child had his or her own nanny. They swam, played tennis, and learned to paint. They were entertained all day long.

While the children played, the women could go to the beauty salon to have their hair done, their nails painted, and so on. There was something for everyone. The restaurants served breakfast, lunch, and dinner. It was a resort where parents could have a vacation as well as the children.

Sojourn with Heidi

When the children were dropped off at 7:00 p.m., they were so tired, but we had to hear about all the things they had done.

During the day I'd find a thatched-roof umbrella with a lawn chair underneath, and my private butler would attend to my every need. The beach went on forever. It was so clean and pristine. Midday, my butler brought me lunch. At 4:00 p.m. he brought me a rum cocktail with some snacks.

Walking the beach and swimming in that turquoise ocean was almost like being in the Virgin Islands. I was reading a good book and thought about my days sailing. It was so relaxing. What a great place! It was one of my best vacations!

Renata was working as a professor in her field, and Scott was working for Google. In 2011 Renata went on sabbatical so she could go to Kingston, Ontario, to the Queen's University. Renata got her PhD at the university and was now working to help other students get their advanced degrees.

Scott was working for Google in Kitchener, Ontario. He rented a place there, and Renata rented a house with Victor in Kingston. This was a tough year for Scott because he commuted every weekend to see his family. Google was very generous with Scott, allowing him to leave on Fridays and drive back on Mondays.

Renata and Scott loved Canada, and Scott loved working for Google. They decided to sell their apartment in Brazil and move to Canada. This was a big change for everyone, including me. Canada was a lot closer to Hilton Head than Brazil!

They found a beautiful house in Waterloo, Ontario. I was happy to help them financially. Victor learned English very fast. He has no accent!

All their belongings were shipped from Brazil, including the fridge I had bought for Scott for when he went to college. Visiting with them in their new home was great. The house had four bedrooms upstairs, and downstairs was a living room, dining room, kitchen, and family room. The great room in the basement was something else again. It was a perfect place for children to play their games on a giant TV screen. There were bunk beds for sleepovers and a computer area with all kinds of games.

They also had a home gym with a treadmill and weights. After your workout, it was only a short walk to the refrigerator for cold drinks. The shower on that level was fabulous. This was a dream home for a young family, with a perfect man cave for the men!

In April 2013, I received more news. Dick Sinn, Janet's husband, passed away on April 27, another sad day.

In June 2013, my stepdaughter Rena invited Scott, Renata, Victor, and me to visit her island in the Thousand Islands on the Canadian side. Rena had divorced her husband a year earlier and now had a new boyfriend. We spent one week there and loved the place.

Rena had two boys. William was eleven years old, and Henry was eight. They had a very nice dog who loved the water. Scott helped by cutting the grass with a small tractor. They also had skidoos, which everyone used. The water was a bit cold in the islands, which is fed from Lake Ontario, but I managed to go swimming almost every day. The house had a firepit, so we had a fire going every day. We all cooked together and had a great time. While we were at the house, something went wrong with the plumbing. Rena and her boyfriend tried to fix the problem but knew it would probably need the assistance of a plumber.

We didn't want to leave, but we all had to get home. We drove back to Waterloo, and I flew back to Hilton Head the following day.

Later that month, I received the most terrifying news. The plumbing issues had continued, so Rena brought a plumber to the island to get the problem fixed. After the plumber completed the project, she took him back to his home. On an island the transportation was all by boat. She took the plumber to his dock, then continued her journey home. Rena knew the river better than anyone I know. It was ten thirty at night and pitch-dark. She knew a shortcut back to her dock and decided to take it. But while driving she unexpectedly had to sway the boat away from a fallen tree. In the process of the maneuver, she hit some rocks and was thrown out of the boat. She suffered a broken neck and did not survive the accident. She died on July 14, 2013.

It was such a shock for everyone. Rena had done everything full speed ahead. There was no in-between. I had to tell Scott and Renata about the accident. They canceled an upcoming flight to Brazil so they could attend the funeral. Everyone was there. It was a very sad day. I felt so sorry for Rena's two young boys—first their parents' divorce and now the loss of their mother. As of this day, I still can't believe it happened.

34

Life Goes On

At home on Hilton Head, I enjoyed the symphony and golf. I bought season tickets for the symphony and plays, and I attended many golf tournaments. Now I wanted to do more traveling.

I gave up working for the Port Royal pro shop. I also gave up being an usher for the orchestra and plays. Working for the Heritage as a Shotlink volunteer was also not my priority anymore. I had done all of those things for almost seven years.

Traveling again was now much more interesting. Australia and New Zealand were at the top of my list. I met a friend's mother in Sidney, and she showed me the best parts of that city. Then I met Debbie, Cal's daughter, in Auckland. We had a picnic in the park with her two children. Hobart was also included.

Alaska out of Vancouver was another great trip. With Bonnie, a skiing friend, I went on several cruises, including one to the Caribbean. I was painting a lot and went to several workshops in Europe, three with Ushi in France and one in Siena, Italy.

I drove from Salzburg, Austria, to my workshop in Italy. My Salzburg friends Horst and Friedegard helped me get there. Horst had a new gadget in his new car and had to test it. It was called a GPS! We all have that now.

The place was up on a hill. It had once been a monastery, and it was magnificent, with a pool and a view to die for! I met a friend from Hilton Head who was registered for the same workshop. What a surprise. It was all very exciting!

All was going well until a horsefly bit me. I broke out with a terrible rash that caused extreme itching. To stop the itch, I decided to paint my watercolor paintings in the pool. The idea may sound crazy, but it was so soothing. It really helped the itch, and I painted whatever I could see around the pool.

The time was passing quickly. Diane, my friend from Hilton Head, and I decided to drive to the Amalfi Coast. That was some drive. With those serpentine roads along the coast and buses all along the way, I never thought we'd make it alive. Finally, we arrived in town and had to find a place to stay. There were no parking spaces anywhere. I stopped in front of a boutique and saw a sign that read "Auberge California." "Okay," I said to Diane, "see if you can get us room?"

As she went across the street, people kept honking at me to move. Finally, she came back and said they had a room for us. Someone from the hotel followed her to tell us where to park.

Parking in such a small area was worth a picture. We had to take our belongings out of the car first because after the car was parked, you could open only one door a bit to get out. Actually, the guy from the hotel parked the car for us.

Now Diane said, "I have bad news and good news." Today we had to sleep in the maid's room, but tomorrow we'd be moved into a beautiful room with a balcony and an ocean view.

The first night was crazy. There was a single bed and a bathtub. I opted to bunk down in the tub. I got a pillow and sheets and a quilt, and somehow it worked.

The next day, all was great! After a great breakfast on the patio, we were shown to our new room. We had a balcony and a view to die for. A hotel doctor looked at my rash and gave me a shot. After two days, everything cleared up. It was such a relief.

The car could not be moved, but being downtown, we could walk everywhere. We went to Capri by ferry and explored everything. I bought a nice linen dress there, which I still have. It was great fun! Then it was time to say *arrivederci* to Amalfi and head back to Rome.

Diane had to get her flight home out of Rome. Everything went well on our trip back until we were outside of Rome. We stopped to talk with a police officer. I showed him our hotel address and explained our situation as best I could in Italian. He told us to follow him. What a scary ride that was, just like a James Bond movie! The officer had his siren blasting and went through all the red lights. I tried to stay right behind him. I was sweating blood, but we survived the trip!

The officer showed us to the hotel. I realized we were on a one-way street going the wrong way. I decided to back up into the location, and that solved the problem. Now there was the parking problem. I pleaded with the hotel manager, "Can I park between the two plants in front of the hotel? It's only for two nights, and I will not move the car." I told him he could place the plants in front of the car so it would be impossible for me to drive the car.

He actually smiled, and with his bad English he agreed. We got it done! I told him I would pay for the parking. The two days in Rome were a blast!

Diane was picked up by taxi at 5:00 a.m. and went off to the airport to get her flight home. I planned to get on my way shortly thereafter.

I hired a taxi to show me how to access the right highway to Austria. Afterward, the hotel staff moved the two plants, and I started on my way to Salzburg so I could return the car on time. I got there on time. The car was thoroughly inspected, and the staff didn't find one scratch on it. This car had gone through a lot, and so had we.

Veronica was waiting for me in Salzburg, and we had a lot of laughs about this trip.

35

My Love for Hilton Head Island

On Hilton Head, I started a ponytail canasta group. The players were Lynn, Darlene, Barbara (Lee's mother), and me. We had many great days playing the game, and some of us still play.

It wasn't all fun and games. I decided to make some changes to my home. I wanted an outside patio. I did the sketch and design of the patio. Doing the project would involve removing ten trees from the area. The trees were removed, then the work could begin. I contacted the contractors who had built the house to get their thoughts on the project. They knew the locations of the underground plumbing and electrical wiring. They knew the locations of all the equipment associated with the pool. I felt safe with their workmanship. It was a big project!

I used old Savannah bricks for the trim and raised the corner area for the outdoor furniture and umbrella. When it was all finished, it looked great! Next, I bought a grill so I could barbecue. I added additional chairs and a two-person bar.

Everything went well, and I loved it. It was great for parties as well as cocktails with a few friends. There originally was just one door from the kitchen to the pool and a sliding door from my bedroom to the patio. I made some changes to that design. I added a side door from the living room so that I could access the patio from my living room. I also added a sliding door from the living room, providing access to the pool and hot tub. All of this was great fun for me. My father was an architect, and I often watched him work. Creating different designs was an exciting challenge for me.

The changes to my home improved on how I used my space. The design was conducive to entertaining small and large groups. Guests could move freely from the pool area to the patio, parlor, and kitchen. The pool and patio area were secured by screens, keeping me and my guests free from unwanted bugs and pests.

I have lived in this house for twenty-one years and continue to make improvements each year. When I had the back patio work done, I also had a fountain installed in the front of the house, the entrance area.

I replaced the EIFS (exterior insulation and finish system) stucco on the house. After a while it was time to re-plaster the pool, another large undertaking. I also added parquet floors and new carpets. Other changes to the house included faux painting the kitchen. There are always things to do in a home, and I love planning and doing the projects!

During Hurricane Matthew in 2016, I had some damage to my property. A big tree fell over and had to be removed from the roof of my garage. I had to fix the garage roof and install a new driveway. I added new cabinets in the garage for additional storage and installed a new garage floor.

I had a large tree removed from the backyard as well as the stub. In this space, I added an outdoor firepit made with Savannah bricks.

I mention all these renovations to highlight the love I have for my home. I am grateful for my good health, my active mind and body, and my continuing desire to take on new challenges every year. I remind my friends that their age is just a number. Keep inspiring yourself to take on new challenges and live with the enthusiasm of a child.

While writing this book, I have had an opportunity to remember the many dear friends I have known and loved over the years.

Cal's passing left me alone. The boat was sold, and then I started to develop new friendships. I have memories of so many fun things I did with my great friends. They, of course, were instrumental in introducing me to the idea of dating again. Dating was fun. I enjoyed going to the movies and dinner.

My friend Jackie introduced me to her cousin Denny. We had so much fun. We traveled to see Mount Rushmore together and Crazy Horse. It's too bad he lives in South Dakota!

My friend Lynne introduced me to Rich. We also traveled together and had a good time. Then Bob and Diane introduced me to Norm, a very nice gentleman from Naples, Florida. We all played tennis together. He wrote beautiful letters to me. I was sad to learn from Bob that Norm passed away. Then there was Steve. We met on a cruise ship, and he visited me at Hilton Head.

Skip and Tina introduced me to Gary, who lived in New Orleans. We all went together to visit him in New Orleans, only to learn that he had been suffering with cancer and had passed away shortly before we arrived. Sad moments for sure, but life goes on.

I would be remiss not to mention my best friend Veronica. We were raised in Salzburg and have been lifelong friends. She is like a sister to me and has been part of my family since we were little girls. Veronica and I have shared the good times and the sad times, including the loss of my mother. Veronica, you are truly my best friend.

I must mention my dear friend Helmut. He is also from Salzburg. He was born in the same clinic as me, by the same midwife. He spent his young life in Salzburg, but we never met until he lived on Hilton Head Island in 2003. We have maintained our friendship over the years, visiting in both Salzburg and Hilton Head.

These two Austrian friends have a special place in my heart.

There were other acquaintances in my past, but those mentioned in this book had a significant impact on me—all dear friends who gave an extra measure of joy to my life.

About four years ago, I met a gentleman here in Hilton Head. My friend John, who skied with our group, had passed away, and his wife Susan invited the ski club members to John's celebration of life. This was where I met Al. I love Al for being such a fine, quality man. He has five children, and I've met them all. They are a bunch of great people! Al and I continue to date and share our lives. We have our own homes but see each other often each week. We enjoy concerts and the theater and sometimes a good movie. He doesn't play golf or tennis anymore. However, I am still very much involved with sports. I play lots of golf and tennis. Al and I enjoy watching sporting events together. He's very special to me, and I treasure our friendship.

I must say that for me life is good! I love Hilton Head, my great friends, the perfect weather (most of the time), and especially being physically well and able to still do the things I enjoy. I am also thankful for my pool! There is nothing like jumping into the pool on the hot, humid summer days on Hilton Head Island!

I would like to say thank you to the person who helped me write my book. My neighbor Barbara Lagorio helped me throughout the process. Besides being the nicest person in the world, she has the patience and willingness to always make time for me. She also made it fun. We discussed the project and my ideas. She said she loved the project because it helped her to work on her computer skills. But mostly, she said she enjoyed my company! It was a learning process for both of us and resulted in a wonderful friendship. We'd meet once a week to edit the document and discuss any new information I had researched and wanted to include in my story. She was so impressed with my collection of years of diaries, photos, and sketches of the islands that I had visited. I had saved all of this material over the years. It was immensely helpful to me as I researched different sections of the book. This made the project so interesting for both of us and kept us laughing! Barbara, thank you again from the bottom of my heart for all your time and the help you gave me.

As you can see, my life experiences have pleased me immensely. My life has been full and rewarding. But the most rewarding aspect has been the wonderful friends I've made along the journey. Just as each island that I visited during my seven years at sea was unique and beautiful, so are each of my friendships. My friends have enriched my life more than I can ever say. I'm a very lucky girl!

About the Author

Heidi Fearon is still living on an island. She is a permanent resident of Hilton Head Island. She loves all that Hilton Head Island has to offer. She is devoted to her son Scott and grandson Victor. Heidi plays golf and tennis. She never misses an opportunity to take on a new challenge. Her interest in painting and fashion persists, and her sewing machine is still her close companion.